ARCHAIC
GREEK POETRY

ARCHAIC GREEK POETRY

An Anthology

Selected and translated by
BARBARA HUGHES FOWLER

THE UNIVERSITY OF WISCONSIN PRESS

The University of Wisconsin Press
1930 Monroe Street
Madison, Wisconsin 53711

3 Henrietta Street
London WC2E 8LU, England

www.wisc.edu\wisconsinpress

2 4 6 7 5 3

Printed in the United States of America

Library of Congress Cataloging-in-Publication Data
Archaic Greek poetry: an anthology / selected and translated by
Barbara Hughes Fowler.
360 pp. cm. — (Wisconsin studies in classics)
Includes bibliographical references (p. 345).
ISBN 0-299-13510-1 (cloth) ISBN 0-299-13514-4 (paper)
1. Greek poetry—Translations into English. I. Fowler, Barbara
Hughes, 1926– II. Series.
PA3622.F69 1992
881'.0108—dc20 92-50251

For A.M.F.

CONTENTS

PREFACE

THE GREEK POETRY of the seventh and sixth centuries B.C. gives us a picture of an aristocratic society that fought its local wars, indulged in political intrigue, and was forever on its guard against the rise of the merchant class and the threat of tyranny, but that for the most part delighted in all that was radiant and delicate. Its poets wrote of flowers, food, and wine; of music, song, and dance; of clothing, jewelry, and scent; of horses, fishes, and birds; and above all of what was, to use one of their own favorite words, *poikilos,* "variegated." They took pleasure in the subtle variations in pitch of flute and lyre, of human and bird song, and in the play of light upon surfaces of all kinds: silver trinkets, golden snake bracelets, birds' plumage, embroidered slippers, fluttering leaves, the sea's surface, wrought cauldrons, the starry sky. Often they described these objects with what we should call color words—green, dark blue, crimson, purple, tawny—but which seem to denote a quality of light rather than specific hues. In my translations I have, however, kept the color words as specific as I could in order to give the poems the archaic flavor I think they should have, even though it may startle a modern audience to hear of a green complexion or a purple sea.

The archaic poets wrote too of the tender flesh of young women and men and of their loves for one another. They also described the ambrosial scent and radiance at the epiphany of one goddess; the profound shudder of nature at the birth of another; the sprouting of a vine upon a ship's mast at still another divine presence. They composed choral odes for young women to dance and sing to goddesses as well as for young men to praise the victors in the games by comparing them to heroes of mythology and so ultimately to the gods. They wrote of the dawn of the world.

I have chosen for this anthology those poems and fragments of poems that I think best exemplify the archaic aesthetic.[1] Of the

1. I have elsewhere described this aesthetic in detail: "The Archaic Aesthetic," *American Journal of Philology* 105 (1984): 119–49.

Homeric Hymns I have selected those that are thought to be of archaic date and that are of interest for their charm of narrative, for their evocation of the magic of nature, and for the sensuous detail in their descriptions of colors, scent, clothing, and jewelry of gold.

Of the elegists and iambicists I have chosen the single surviving poem of Kallinos and one poem of Tyrtaios to represent the martial spirit of the age. Semonides' long poem, not to be taken too seriously, represents the misogyny that elsewhere more subtly characterizes early Greek literature. Mimnermos exemplifies both the pessimism of the archaic period and, in his mythological poems, its lyric incandescence. Solon's Prayer to the Muses (13) is significant for its clustering of the tragic concepts of *olbos-hybris-ate* (prosperity-violence-ruin) and *dike* (justice), and for its statement, also presaging the tragic poets, that the sins of the fathers will be visited upon the children even unto the third generation. Theognis represents the dismay of the aristocrats in the late archaic period at the rise of the merchant class and the consequent threat of tyranny.

I have translated almost every fragment of Archilochos, and the one poem of Hipponax that was once attributed to him, because I think that he will in his great variety appeal to a modern audience. There are love poems and fragments of fables; poems of friendship and warfare, of colonization and homesickness; poems that are delicate, humorous, and often, by modern standards, obscene.

Of the lyricists I have translated virtually every fragment, for indeed fragments are, with one or two exceptions, all that remain of this corpus, which is made up of papyrus fragments and quotations in other authors, who cite these poets often only to illustrate a point of meter, grammar, or dialect. We rarely therefore have a context for the quotation, and the *poikilia* of these poets is known to us in large part from broken lines and sometimes from one-word fragments, such as Alkman 127, "earring." It is perhaps the tantalizingly fragmentary nature of these poems that makes them so enchanting to us.

Of Bakchylides and Pindar I have chosen those odes which are most appealing for the myths they relate and for the luminosity of their presentation. These poems are difficult chiefly for the bewildering array of proper names they present and sometimes for the allusive nature of the narrative, but the reader who will patiently use the Notes and the Glossary of Proper Names should have little trouble in understanding these most iridescent of poems.

The Greek language is strong in vowels; English, in consonants. Greek prefers falling rhythms; English, rising rhythms. Greek verse is quantitative; English, accentual. Greek also had a pitch accent which did not affect the meter but which did give another whole dimension to the sound of the verse. Greek because of its many prefixes, infixes, and suffixes could create long polysyllabic words, and these together with its vast array of particles allowed a poet to compose a long but light line expressing what an English poet must often express in fewer syllables and with fewer metrical feet. For these reasons I have not attempted in these translations to reproduce the meters of the original poems, although I have in the case of all the complete poems and longer fragments of poems tried to preserve the look of the poem upon the page. It seemed to me best to make English poems in English meters out of the Greek poems, while at the same time being as faithful to the sense of the Greek text as I possibly could.

I have not been entirely consistent in my transliteration of Greek names. For the most part I have kept the Greek spellings, but for a few very familiar names, such as Achilles, Ajax, Athens, Thebes, and Corinth, I have used the conventional Anglicized forms. Line numbers where they occur refer to the Greek texts.

I have used the following texts: D. B. Monroe and T. W. Allen, *Homeri Opera* (Oxford, 1946); M. L. West, *Iambi et Elegi Graeci*, 2 vols. (Oxford, 1971); D. L. Page, *Poetae Melici Graeci* (Oxford, 1962); Page, *Supplementum Lyricis Graecis* (Oxford, 1974); E. Lobel and D. L. Page, *Poetarum Lesbiorum Fragmenta* (Oxford, 1955); B. Snell and H. Maehler, *Bacchylides* (Leipzig, 1970); B. Snell and H. Maehler, *Pindarus*, 2 vols. (Leipzig, 1975, 1980). I have also consulted E. Voigt, *Sappho et Alcaeus* (Amsterdam, 1971). I have cited testimonia from D. A. Campbell, *Greek Lyric*, vols. 1 and 2 (Cambridge, Mass., 1982, 1988); J. M. Edmonds, *Lyra Graeca*, 3 vols. (Cambridge, Mass., 1959, 1963, 1964).

HOMERIC HYMNS

II

Hymn to Demeter

I begin to sing of Demeter of the lovely hair,
revered goddess, of her and her delicate-ankled daughter
whom Aidoneus seized, and Zeus who sees wide, god
of the deep thunder, gave her to him. Apart from her mother,
Demeter of sword of gold and glorious fruits, she played
with the full-breasted daughters of Ocean, culling blossoms, the rose
and crocus and lovely violets over the soft meadow,
irises and hyacinths, the narcissus too,
which Gaia made grow as a snare for the girl of flowering face
by the will of Zeus to favor the Host of Many Souls,
a wondrous radiant bloom, a marvel for all to see,
whether they were immortal gods or mortal men.
From its root there grew a hundred blossoming heads
of sweetest scent so that all the broad heaven above
and all the earth laughed and the salt swell of the sea.
The girl was amazed and stretched forth both her hands to grasp
the lovely toy, but the wide-wayed earth gaped
in the Nysian plain, and then the lord, Host of Many,
with immortal horses, leapt upon her, Kronos' son
of many names. He snatched her up against her will
upon his golden chariot and carried her off
crying lamentably. She shrieked with piercing voice,
and called upon her father, son of Kronos, best
and supreme, but no immortal god or mortal man
heard her voice, nor gleaming-fruited olive trees.
Only Persaios' daughter of tender intent heard
from her cave, Hekate of splendid diadem.
There heard as well the lord Helios, glorious son
of Hyperion, as she called upon her father, son
of Kronos, but he was sitting apart from the other gods
in his temple where many come to beseech and was accepting
lovely offerings from mortal men, and so

30–68 Kronos' son of many names, Commander and Host
of Many, her own uncle, carried her off upon
his immortal car, at Zeus' behest, against her will.
As long as the goddess looked upon the land and sky
sparkling with stars and the rolling sea where fishes shoal
and the rays of the sun, still she hoped to see her revered
mother and the tribes of the everlasting gods, and hope
soothed her great soul although she was distressed.
The mountain peaks and the depths of the sea echoed with
her immortal voice, and her lady mother heard her cry.
Piercing pain seized at her heart, and she tore about
her ambrosial locks with her dear hands her diadem
and cast down from both her shoulders her blue-black cloak
and sped like a bird of prey over the dry land
and the wet seas, searching. But no one was willing to tell
to her the truth, neither god nor mortal man,
nor did there come to her as truthful messenger
any bird. For nine days then did the lady Deo
roam the earth with blazing torches held in hand,
nor once did she taste ambrosia or nectar's sweet drink
in her distress, nor did she bathe her flesh, but when
the tenth and shining dawn had come upon her,
Hekate encountered her; she carried a torch
and as a messenger spoke and said to her this:
"Lady Demeter, bringer of seasons and glorious gifts,
who of the heavenly gods or who of mortal men
has snatched Persephone and grieved your dear soul?
I heard her voice but did not see with my own eyes
who it was. Quickly I tell you all the truth."
So, then, Hekate spoke, but Rhea's lovely-haired
daughter answered not a word but sped with her,
holding blazing torches in her hands. They came
to Helios, who watched both gods and men, and stood
before his steeds, and the shining of goddesses asked him this:
"Do you, Helios, at least, respect me, a goddess,
if ever by word or deed I have warmed your heart or soul.
Through the barren sky I heard the shrill cry of the daughter
I bore, my sweet shoot, illustrious in form,
as though she were raped, though I did not see with my own eyes,

but you, for you with your beams behold all the land
and the sea from the shining ether above, truthfully
tell me about my child. Have you seen her anywhere?
Who of gods or mortal men has seized her by force
against her will and mine and so made off with her?"
So she spoke. The son of Hyperion answered her:
"Daughter of Rhea of lovely hair, Demeter queen,
you shall know. I respect and pity you very much
in your anguish for your delicate-ankled daughter. No other
of immortal gods is to blame but the cloud-gatherer Zeus,
who gave her to Hades, his own brother, to be named
his blossoming bride. He snatched and took her upon his car
beneath the misty dark as she shouted out, but,
goddess, stop your enormous moaning. It is not right
to keep in vain your unrelenting anger. Aidoneus,
Commander of Many, is not an unfit bridegroom
among immortals, your own brother of the same stock.
He has for honor that third share of the first division
and dwells among those whose king he happens by lot to be."
So he spoke and summoned his steeds, and at his bidding
nimbly they bore the swift car like long-winged birds.
But pain more savage and terrible still came to her heart,
and angered with the son of Kronos of black clouds,
she afterward went apart from the gods' assembly and steep
Olympos to the cities and rich fields of men,
for a long time defacing her beautiful form. No one
of men or full-bosomed women who looked recognized her
until she came to the house of prudent Keleus, who
was at that time king of fragrant Eleusis. She sat
near the road, grieved at her dear heart, beside
the Maiden Well, where the city's women drew their water,
in a shady spot where a shrub of olive grew above,
and she was like an ancient old woman, deprived
of childbirth and the gifts of garlanded Aphrodite,
like the nurse of royal children dispensing justice, or like
the housekeepers in their echoing halls. There the daughters
of Keleus, son of Eleusis, saw her as they came
to fetch the water, easily drawn, to carry it
in pitchers of bronze to their father's dear house. Four

108–144 were they, like goddesses, in blossoming girlhood,
Kallidike, Kleisidike, and lovely Demo, and Kallithoe,
who was the eldest of them all. They did not know
the goddess, for gods are difficult for mortals to see,
but standing nearby they spoke to her with winged words:
"Who are you, old woman, of those born long before?
Where are you from? Why have you walked apart from the town
and not approached the house? For there in the shadowy halls
are women of just your age and some who are younger, and they
would welcome and cherish you in both their words and their
deeds."
So they spoke, and the queen of goddesses replied,
"My dear children, whoever you are of womankind,
I greet you, and I will tell you my tale, for not
unseemly is it to tell you truly what you ask.
Doso is my name, my lady mother's choice.
And now from Crete over the broad back of the sea
I have come, not willingly, but pirates forcibly
brought me away against my will, and afterward
with their swift ship they put in at Thorikos.
Then the women disembarked upon the shore
in throngs, and the men too, and they prepared a meal
beside the cables of the ship. But I had no heart
for the sweet supper they made, but stealthily I fled
hasting across the black land and so escaped
violent masters that they not sail with me across
the sea and get a price they had not paid for me.
And so, wandering, I have come here, nor do
I know at all what land this is nor who they are
who live in it, but may all who have their homes upon
Olympos grant you husbands to wed and birth of children,
as parents desire. Pity me, maidens, in turn.
Kindly [give me this clear advice in order that I
may learn,] my dear girls, to the house of what man
or woman I may go that I may work for them
gladly at tasks befitting a woman of my age.
Holding a newborn child in my arms I could nurse him well
or keep the house or spread my master's bed in a nook
of a well-constructed room and teach the women their work."

The goddess spoke. Straightway the unwed girl replied, 145–182
Kallidike, the loveliest of all of Keleus' daughters:
"Mother, the gifts of the gods, though grieved, we mortals must
endure, for they are stronger by far than we. But now
I shall give you clearly this advice, and I shall name
the men who have great power and honor here and are
preeminent among the people and with their counsel
and straight decrees protect our city's battlements:
Triptolemos, the shrewd, and Diokles, Polyxeinos,
Eumolpos the blameless, Dolichos, and our manly father.
All these have wives who manage their household affairs. Of them
not one, after first sight of you, would turn you from
the house in disrespect, but they will welcome you,
for you are like a god. But if you wish, remain
here, that we may go to my father's house and tell
Metaneira, our full-breasted mother, all of this straight through
to see whether she will bid you to come to our house
rather than seek the homes of other men. She has
an only late-born son, nursed in our well-built house,
an answer to many prayers and cherished. If you could rear
this child until he reached the full measure of youth,
anyone of womankind, seeing you,
would easily be envious, such gifts would she,
our mother, give you for your nurturing of him."
So she spoke, and the goddess nodded her head in assent.
They filled their shining pails with water and carried them off
with pride. Swiftly they came to their father's great house
and quickly told their mother what they had seen and heard.
She bade them go and summon with all speed the stranger
for a limitless wage. As heifers or hinds in the season of spring
bound about the meadow, their hearts sated with pasture,
so they, holding up the folds of their lovely dresses,
darted down the hollow wagon path, and their hair
leapt about their shoulders like the blossoming crocus cup.
They found the stately goddess beside the road where they
had left her before, but now they brought her to the house
of their dear father. She walked behind with her head veiled,

182–217 sorrowing in her heart. Her blue-black cloak
wove about the goddess's delicate feet as she walked.
Straightway they came to the house of god-nurtured Keleus
and went through the portico to where their lady mother
sat beside a support of the closely compacted roof,
holding her child in her lap, her newborn tender shoot.
Her daughters ran to her, and the goddess stepped upon
the threshold. Her head touched the roof and she filled the door
with a heavenly radiance. Then reverence and awe seized
upon Metaneira and pale fear, and she yielded her chair
and bade the goddess sit. But Demeter who brings the seasons
and glorious gifts did not wish to sit upon
the gleaming couch but remained silent with her lovely eyes
downcast until well-mannered Iambe set for her
a joined seat and cast upon it a silvery fleece.
There she sat and held her veil before her face.
For a long time in sorrowing silence she sat upon
the chair, nor did she welcome anyone by word
or deed, but unsmiling, tasting neither food nor drink,
she sat, wasting in longing for her full-breasted daughter,
until well-mannered Iambe with jokes and many a jest
persuaded the holy lady to smile and laugh and have
a cheerful heart. She pleased her temper afterward too.
Metaneira offered her a cup which she had filled
with honey-sweet wine but she nodded refusal, for she said,
it was not permitted her to drink red wine but bade
them mix water and barley meal with soft mint
and give it to her to drink. Metaneira mixed the potion
and offered it to the goddess as she had bade, and Deo,
the very august, accepted it as a sacrament.

. . . .

Of them Metaneira, beautifully sashed, began to speak:
"I greet you, lady, for I do not suppose that you
are of humble parentage, but noble, for dignity
and grace are obvious in your countenance as in those
of kings who administer laws. But the gifts of the gods, though grieved,
we mortals bear perforce. For on our necks there lies

a yoke. But now, since you have come here, you 218–251
shall have all that I can provide. Nurse for me
this child whom the immortal gods offered to me
late born and beyond my expectation, an answer
to many prayers. If you could rear this child until
he should reach the full measure of youth, anyone
of womankind, seeing you, would easily
be envious. Such gifts should I give to you in return
for your nurturing." Beautifully crowned Demeter replied,
"And greetings, my woman, to you, and the gods' favor too.
Gladly will I accept the child, as you ask me,
and I will nurse him and never do I expect that through
his nurse's carelessness witchcraft shall hurt him
or even the Undercutter, for I know a medicine
stronger by far than the Cutter of Wood, the toothache worm,
and a strong antidote to ward off witchcraft."
So she spoke and took the child to her fragrant breast
with her immortal hands, and his mother rejoiced in her heart.
So in his halls the goddess nursed Demophoön,
prudent Keleus' glorious son whom beautifully sashed
Metaneira bore. He grew like some divinity,
for he ate not food nor did he drink [of his mother's milk],
for by day Demeter, beautifully crowned, anointed him
with ambrosia as though he were the offspring of a god
and breathed upon him sweetly, holding him to her breast.
By night she would hide him like a brand in the fire's heart
in secret from his dear parents, who were much amazed
at his precocious growth. For he was like the gods,
to encounter. And she would have made him unaging and deathless too,
had not beautifully sashed Metaneira foolishly
kept her watch by night from her fragrant marriage chamber
and spied. But she shrieked and struck both her thighs in fear
for her child, and she was terribly distraught in her soul,
and so she wept and wailed and uttered winged words:
"Demophoön, my child, the stranger conceals you
deep in fire and causes me grief and bitter woes."
So she spoke, lamenting, and the shining of goddesses,
beautifully crowned Demeter, heard and was angered at her.

252–289 The dear son, whom she had borne beyond her hope
in the halls, she dashed with her immortal hands to the ground,
snatched from the fire, for she was terribly wroth in her heart.
At the same time she spoke to beautifully sashed Metaneira:
"Mortal men are ignorant and witless to know
in advance their approaching fate, whether evil or good.
For you, infatuate, have wrought incurable folly.
For, let the oath of the gods know, the implacable water
of Styx, I would have made your child unaging and deathless
for all his days and bestowed honor imperishable
upon him, but now it is impossible for him
to escape death and the fates, but imperishable honor
shall always be his because he lay upon my knees
and slumbered in my arms, but as the seasons go by,
the sons of the Eleusinians will wage war
and terrible battle with one another forevermore.
I am Demeter, who have my share of honor, to mortals
and gods alike the greatest of helps and causes of joy.
But come, let the people build for me a great shrine
and an altar below it beneath the steep citadel
above the spring Kallichoros upon a thrusting hill.
I myself will teach my rites that afterward,
piously performing them, you appease my soul."
When she had spoken so, the goddess changed her stature
and form and thrust old age away. Beauty breathed
about her, and a lovely fragrance spread from her sweet-smelling robes,
and from the immortal flesh of the goddess there shone afar
a light, and her tawny locks covered over her shoulders,
and the sturdy house was filled with a flashing as though of lightning,
and she went away from the halls. Metaneira's knees gave way,
nor did she remember to take from the ground her late-born son,
but his sisters heard his piteous cry and leapt down
from their well-spread beds. And then one of them took
the child in her arms and held him to her bosom; the other
rekindled the fire. The third sped with delicate feet
to rouse and bring their mother from her fragrant room.
They gathered about and bathed the gasping babe and embraced

him lovingly, but his soul was not soothed, because
clumsier nurses and fosterers were handling him now.
All night long they besought the glorious goddess, and quaked
with fear, but with the shining dawn, they told Keleus,
wide in strength, everything unerringly,
as the goddess, Demeter, beautifully crowned, had commanded them.
He called his countless folk to assembly and bade them
construct an opulent shrine to Demeter of the lovely hair
and an altar upon a thrusting hill. They obeyed him
straightway and heard him as he spoke and they built as he
had commanded. The child thrived like some divinity.
But when they had completed and drawn back from their toil,
they went each to his own home, but blond Demeter,
sitting there apart from all the blessed gods,
stayed, wasting with yearning for her full-breasted daughter.
She caused upon the all-nourishing earth a terrible year,
most horrible for mortal men. The soil would not
send up its seed, for Demeter, beautifully crowned, kept
it hid. Many a bent plow oxen drew
in the fields, fruitlessly, and much white barley fell
in vain to the ground. And now she would have destroyed all
the race of articulate men by grievous famine, depriving
those who live upon Olympos of glorious right
of gifts and sacrifice, had Zeus not noted this
and marked it in his heart. First he sped Iris
of golden wings to summon Demeter of beautiful hair
who has the very lovely form. So he spoke.
And she obeyed Zeus of the black clouds, the son
of Kronos; her feet covered swiftly the distance between. She came
to the citadel of fragrant Eleusis, and found in her temple
Demeter who wears the blue-black cloak, and she spoke to her
and addressed her there in winged words and said this:
"Demeter, father Zeus of imperishable wisdom
summons you to come to the tribes of the eternal gods,
so come and let not my word from Zeus be unfulfilled."
So she spoke, beseechingly, but did not persuade
Demeter's heart. The father next sent forth all

325–363 the blessed and immortal gods, and, coming each in turn,
they kept calling and offered many beautiful gifts
and whatever honors she might choose to take among
the immortal gods, but none could persuade her mind or her wits,
so wroth was her soul. Stubbornly she rejected their words.
For never, she said, would she step upon fragrant Olympos
nor allow fruit to spring from the earth until she beheld
with her own eyes her daughter who had the lovely face.
    But when wide-seeing Zeus of the deep thunder heard this,
he sent to Erebos Argeïphontes of golden wand
so that, persuading Hades with soothing words, he might
bring forth from the misty dark chaste Persephone
to the light to join the divinities so that her mother
might see with her own eyes and so cease from her wrath.
Hermes did not disobey but leapt down and sped
to the hollows beneath the earth, abandoning the seat
of Olympos. He found Hades the lord within his house,
sitting upon a couch with his modest bride who was
reluctant because she longed so for her mother, but she
was far away, devising a terrible plot because
of the deeds of the gods. Standing close beside him,
mighty Argeïphontes spoke to him and said,
    "Hades of the blue-black hair, who rule the perished dead,
Zeus the father bids me bring forth from Erebos
to them the noble Persephone that her mother may see
with her own eyes and so cease from her terrible wrath
and anger with the deathless gods. For she plots to destroy
the strengthless tribes of earthborn men by hiding the seed
beneath the soil and destroying so the honors owed
to the undying gods, for she cherishes a terrible wrath
and mingles not with the gods but sits apart within
her fragrant shrine in Eleusis' rocky citadel."
    So he spoke, and Aidoneus, lord of the shades, smiled
with a lift of his brows, but he obeyed the commands of Zeus
the king and hastily bade prudent Persephone,
    "Persephone, go to your mother of the blue-black cloak,
keeping a kindly spirit and soul within your breast
nor be exceedingly dispirited, for I
shall be among the deathless gods a husband not

unfitting for you, for I am brother to father Zeus,
and while you are here, you shall be queen of everything
that lives and creeps and have the greatest honors among
the immortal gods. Vengeance will come for all their days
to those who do you wrong and fail to appease your might
with sacrifices and rites, piously performed,
and to those who fail to honor you with fitting gifts."
    So he spoke, and prudent Persephone rejoiced
and quickly leapt up for joy, but he, secretly,
gave her to eat the honey-sweet pomegranate seed,
arranging for himself that she not remain for all
her days with grave Demeter of the blue-black cloak.
Aidoneus, Commander of Many, prepared close by to yoke
his immortal steeds beneath his golden chariot.
    She mounted the chariot and strong Argeïphontes
took the reins and the whip in his own hands and drove
forth from the halls, and the horses flew, willingly,
and lightly accomplished the long course. Neither the sea
nor river waters nor grassy dells nor mountain peaks
checked the headlong rush of those immortal steeds,
but they sheared the deep ether above as they galloped along.
Hermes brought them to where Demeter, beautifully crowned,
lingered and halted them before her fragrant temple.
Seeing them, she darted forth as does a maenad
down a shadowy mountainside. Persephone,
on the other side, seeing her mother's sweet eyes,
abandoned the chariot and steeds. She leapt and ran
to her and fell upon her neck in fond embrace.
But while Demeter still held her dear child in her arms,
her spirit suddenly suspected some snare,
and she feared terribly and ceased from her affection
and asked all at once, "Child, you did not, I hope,
taste of food while you were below. Speak out. Do not
conceal the truth that we both may know, for if not,
returning from loathsome Hades, you shall live with me
and your father, the son of Kronos, lord of the black clouds,
and you shall be honored among all the immortal gods.
But if you have tasted of food, going back again
to the hollows of earth, you shall dwell there a third part

of the seasons of every year, but for two you shall live with me
and the other immortal gods. But when the earth blooms
with fragrant buds of spring of every variety,
then again from the misty dark you shall rise
to be a great marvel to gods and mortal men.
But tell me how he snatched you away to the misty dark
and by what snare did the Host of Many beguile you?"

The very lovely Persephone answered her in turn:
"I will tell you, mother, everything unerringly.
When the helper Hermes came, the swift messenger,
from my father, Kronos' son, and the other Ouranidai,
to bid me come from Erebos that you might see
and cease from your terrible anger and wrath with the deathless gods,
straightway I leapt up for joy, but he in secret
forced upon me a pomegranate seed,
sweet food, and compelled me to taste against my will.
And how he snatched me away by the shrewd plan of the son
of Kronos, my father, and carried me to the hollows of earth,
I will tell, and I will go through it all, just as you ask.
All of us were playing in a lovely meadow—
Leukippe, Phaino, Elektra, and Ianthe,
Melite, Iache, Rhodeia, and Kallirhoe,
Melobosis and Tyche and Okyroe with face
like a flower, Chryseis, Ianeira, Akeste,
Rhodope, Plouto, and lovely Kalypso, Ourania
and Styx and charming Galaxaura, and Pallas Athena,
the battle-rouser, and Artemis, who delights in arrows—
and plucking lovely blossoms, tender crocuses
mixed with irises and hyacinths and buds
of rose and lilies, a marvel to see, and narcissus too,
which the broad earth made grow, yellow as crocus cup,
and I culled these for joy, but the earth beneath gave way,
and there the lord, the strong Host of Many, leapt forth
and carried me off beneath the earth in his golden car
much against my will. I cried with shrill voice.
Distressed that I am to tell it, all that I say is true."

So then all day long with single passion and thought
they cheered one another's hearts and souls with frequent embrace,

and their spirits ceased from grief, and they gave and received from one
another joyfulness. There came near to them
Hekate of gleaming diadem, who often
embraced Demeter's sacred daughter. From that time
the queen was attendant companion to Persephone.
To them wide-seeing Zeus of the deep thunder sent
as messenger Rhea of the lovely hair to bring Demeter
of the blue-black cloak back to the tribes of the gods.
He promised to give her whatever honors she might choose
among the immortal gods and nodded assent to
her daughter's going below to the misty dark for
a third part of the circling year, and for two parts
living above with her mother and other immortal gods.
So he spoke, and the goddess obeyed the message of Zeus.
Swiftly she darted down from the peaks of Olympos and came
to Rharion, fostering breast of the land in time before
but then not fertile at all but useless and utterly leafless,
for the white barley grain lay hidden by design
of delicate-ankled Demeter. But afterward it would
be tasseled with the slender ears of grain when spring
waxed full, and on the ground the rich furrows would be
weighted with ears while others were bound by cords in sheaves.
There first she stepped from the barren upper air. Gladly
the goddesses saw one another and so rejoiced in their souls,
and Rhea of the gleaming diadem spoke to her:
"Come, my child, for wide-seeing Zeus of the deep thunder
calls you to come to the tribes of the gods and promises you
whatever honors you may choose to have among
the immortal gods and has nodded assent to your daughter's descent
to the misty dark for a third part of the circling year
with two parts for you and the other immortal gods.
So he has said it will be and nodded his head in assent.
But come, my child, and obey, and be not excessively
and unrelentingly angry with Zeus of the black clouds
but increase straightway the fostering fruit for mortal men."
So she spoke. Nor did Demeter, beautifully crowned,
disobey but straightway made the fruit spring up
from the fields of fertile clods so that all the wide earth

472–495 was weighted with leaves and blossoming buds, and going to
the kings who administer the laws she showed Triptolemos
and Diokles, the driver of horses, and mighty Eumolpos
and Keleus, the people's leader, how to perform her rites
and taught to all her mysteries, Triptolemos,
Polyxeinos, and Diokles too, awesome mysteries
which none may transgress nor inquire about nor utter at all,
for mighty awe of the gods holds the voice in check.
Blessed is he of men on earth who has beheld
these rites, but that man who is uninitiate
and has no share of them has no lot of the like
once he has died and gone to the misty dark below.

But when the shining of goddesses had taught them all,
they went to Olympos and to the assembly of other gods,
and there they dwell beside Zeus who delights in thunder,
revered and awesome goddesses. Greatly blessed
of men on earth is he whom they readily love.
Straightway do they send as a hearth-guest to his great house
Ploutos who gives to mortal men enormous wealth.

But, come, you who keep the people of fragrant Eleusis
and Paros, washed by the sea, and rocky Antron, lady
of glorious gifts, bringer of seasons, Deo queen,
you and your daughter, the very lovely Persephone,
graciously for my song bestow sustenance
to cheer, and I will remember you and another song.

IV

Hymn to Hermes

Sing of Hermes, Muse, son of Zeus and Maia,
of Kyllene lord and of Arkadia rich in flocks,
the immortals' helpful messenger whom Maia bore,
the nymph of lovely hair, lying in love with Zeus,
bashfully, for she shunned the company of the blessed
and dwelt in a shaded cave where the son of Kronos lay
with the nymph of lovely hair in the depth of night as long
as sweet sleep embraced Hera of ivory arms,
escaping the ken of immortal gods and mortal men.
But when the intent of mighty Zeus became fulfilled
and the tenth month for her was fixed in heaven above,
then she brought him to birth and remarkable deeds occurred,
for she bore then a beguiling child of many wiles,
a plunderer, a robber of cattle, a bringer of dreams,
a scout by night, a thief at the gate, who was about
to reveal deeds of renown among the immortal gods.
Born with the dawn, by high noon he played the lyre;
at evening he stole the Far-archer Apollo's cows,
on the fourth day of the month when Maia gave him birth.
He, as soon as he leapt from his mother's immortal limbs,
no longer lay in his sacred cradle, lingering,
but leapt up to seek the cattle of Apollo,
stepping above the threshold of the high-roofed cave.
There he found a tortoise, possession of endless delight,
for Hermes was first to make the tortoise a bard, when she
encountered him there at the courtyard doors where she fed upon
the luxuriant grass before the house, waddling along.
The son of Zeus, the helpful messenger, when he spied
the creature laughed and straightway spoke this word and said,
"Already an omen of great profit to me—nor do
I despise it. Hail, my friend of the feast, so lovely in shape,
to strike up the dance! How delighted I am to see you!
Where did you get that lovely gaud, your speckled shell—

a mountain-dwelling tortoise like you? I'll pick you up
and take you inside the house. You'll be of use to me,
nor will I dishonor you, but you will profit me first.
You're better off at home. It's dangerous outdoors.
Alive, you'll charm away mischievous witchcraft,
but if you die, you'll be a very lovely bard."
  So he spoke, and, taking her up in both his hands,
he carried back inside the house his charming toy.
Then with chisel of gray iron he bored through
and scooped from the shell the mountain tortoise's very life.
As swift thought passes through the breast of a man whom
thronging concerns beset, or again as when from the eyes
sparkling glances flash, so did glorious Hermes
devise word and deed instantaneously.
Cutting to measure stalks of reed, he fixed them,
knotting the ends across the back and through the sides
of the tortoise shell, and cunningly stretched around it all
the hide of an ox. He put in the horns and affixed to them
the crosspiece and stretched across from side to side
seven harmonious strings of sheep gut. But when
he had fashioned it, he lifted up his charming toy
and with plectrum tried it string by string. At the touch of his hand
it resounded wondrously. To make trial of it
the god sang a soft and pretty little song,
extemporaneously, as when youths at festivals
taunt offhandedly, about Zeus, and Maia,
beautifully sandaled, and of their dalliance before
in companionship of love, and told the glorious tale
of his own begetting. He celebrated too the maids
and shining home of the nymph, the tripods throughout the house,
the abundant cauldrons too. He sang then these things,
but his mind was otherwise intent. Lifting up
the hollow lyre, he laid it in his sacred cradle.
Then craving for flesh, he leapt from the fragrant megaron
to a lookout place and pondered sheer devilry
with his wits, like robber men in the depths of black night.
  The sun was going down toward Ocean beneath the earth

together with his horses and chariot, but Hermes
came running to the shadowy hills of Pieria
where the blessed gods' immortal cattle kept their steads
and grazed the lovely meadows that were all unshorn.
Of these then the son of Maia Argeïphontes,
keen of sight, cut off from the herd fifty cows,
lowing loud, and drove them aslant through a sandy spot,
turning their tracks aside. He thought of a tricky device,
reversing the prints of their hooves, the first behind, behind
the fore, while he himself proceeded the other way.
Then with wickerwork he wove beside the sands
of the sea sandals, marvelous works, unthought of before,
and unimagined, for he mingled twigs of tamarisk
with myrtle and bound together an armful of fresh growth
and tied securely beneath his feet nimble sandals,
leaves and all, which glorious Argeïphontes plucked,
shunning the path from Pieria, improvising
like one hastening upon a long road.
But an old man, cultivating his blossoming vineyard,
noticed him as he hurried down the plain and through
grassy Onchestos. Maia's very illustrious son
spoke and addressed him first, and this is what he said:
　　"Old man who dig your vines with shoulders bent,
much wine will you surely have when all these plants bear fruit,
if you fail to see what you have seen and are deaf too
to what you have heard and silent about what harms you not."
　　So much he said and rushed the stalwart cattle along
together and drove them through many shadowy hills
and echoing hollows and flowering plains—the glorious Hermes.
The divine night, his dark assistant, was almost gone,
and dawn that sets the people to work was coming on.
Shining Selene, daughter of Pallas, Megamedes'
son, had just mounted her lookout post when
the sturdy son of Zeus drove the wide-browed cows
of Phoibos Apollo toward the river Alpheus, and they,
unwearied, came to the high-roofed fold and the watering troughs
that stood before the splendid meadow. And then when
he had pastured on fodder the cattle, bellowing loud,
and herded them together in throngs into the fold,

107–142 feeding upon the lotus and dewy galingale,
he fetched a load of wood and sought the skill of fire.
Taking a gleaming twig of laurel, he peeled it
with a knife . . .
held tight in his hand, and a hot blast of flame breathed forth,
for Hermes first delivered fire and fire-sticks.
Taking many seasoned logs, he piled them thick
and abundantly in a sunken pit, and a spark glowed
and shot afar a streak of fiercely blazing fire.
And while the might of famous Hephaistos kindled the flame,
he dragged two horned and lowing kine outside and close
beside the fire, for he was possessed of enormous strength.
He hurled them both panting upon their backs to the ground.
Rolling them over, their necks back, he pierced their spines.
Task upon task, he hacked the rich and fatted meat.
He pierced and roasted upon wooden spits the flesh
and honorable chine and black blood within the gut,
all together, and laid them there upon the ground.
The hides he stretched upon a rough and rugged rock,
and they are still there after all these many years
and have been, continuously. But after this
the merry-hearted Hermes dragged the rich meat
to a smoothed flat stone and divided it into twelve shares,
distributed by lot, with perfect honor for each.
Then glorious Hermes longed for the sacrificial flesh,
for the pleasant savor wore him down, immortal though
he was, but his noble heart was not persuaded to eat
the sacrificial flesh, though he desired it much.
But he put away into the high-roofed fold the fat
and much flesh and he hung them high in the air to show
as tokens of his youthful theft. Then taking dry wood,
he destroyed with blast of flame all the hooves and all
the heads. And when the god had accomplished everything
according to need, he cast his sandals into the Alpheus
of deep eddies, quenched the embers, and leveled with sand
the black ash all the night by the lovely light
of Selene. Straightway he returned to the peaks of Kyllene at dawn,
nor did there encounter him upon the long road

anyone of the blessed gods or mortal men,
nor did dogs bark. The son of Zeus, the helpful Hermes,
slipped edgewise through the keyhole of the megaron
like the mist or autumn breeze. Going straight through
the cave he came to the inner room, treading lightly,
making no noise upon the floor. Then glorious Hermes
sped to his cradle and wrapped his swaddling clothes about
his shoulders as though he were a helpless babe and lay
playing with the coverlet about his knees,
though he kept at his left hand his lovely tortoise shell,
but the god did not escape his goddess mother, who said,
"What's this, contriver of wiles? From where do you come, clothed
in shamelessness at this hour of night? I think that the son
of Leto will have you soon outside beneath his hands
and bound about the ribs with irresistible cords,
or you will lead a robber's life in mountain glens.
Off with you again! Your father begat you to be
an enormous worry to mortal men and immortal gods."
Hermes answered her with cunning words and said,
"Mother, why do you attack me like this as though
I were an infant child who knew in his heart a few
mischievous deeds and, frightened, feared his mother's reproof?
But I will embark upon whatever plan is best
to nourish and feed you and me continuously,
nor will we endure, remaining here, as you command,
to be alone among immortal gods without
offerings or prayers. Better all our days
dalliance with the deathless gods and opulence
and wealth and many stores of grain than sitting in
a murky cave for home. As far as honor goes,
I too will enter upon Apollo's holy rite.
And if my father refuses it to me, then I
will try—and I can—to be a chief of robber men.
And if Leto's very famous son should seek me out,
I think that something else, a bigger loss still,
will befall him. For I shall go to Pytho to bore
straight through his mighty home and steal from there enough
exceedingly lovely tripods, cauldrons, and gold, and enough

180–216 gleaming iron and clothes, and you shall see if you will."
So with these words they spoke with one another,
the son of aegis-bearing Zeus and the lady Maia.
Now early-born Dawn was bringing to mortals light
as she rose from the depths of the rolling Ocean when Apollo went
and came to Onchestos, the very lovely and holy grove
of the loudly roaring Earth-upholder. There he found
an ancient man grazing his beast along the path
from his vineyard, and Leto's glorious son addressed him first:
"Old man, plucker of thorns from grassy Onchestos,
I have come here from Pieria in search of cattle,
all of them cows, all with crumpled horns, from my herd.
The black bull was feeding alone apart from the rest,
but gleaming-eyed dogs followed behind, four of them,
of single mind, like men. But they were left behind,
the dogs and the bull, which was a wonder, but the cows,
just as the sun was sinking down, strayed away
from the soft meadow and from the sweet pasturage.
Tell me, old man, born long ago, if anywhere
you've seen a man pursuing a path behind these cows."
The old man answered him in words and said this:
"It is difficult, O friend, to tell all that my eyes
have seen, for many travelers take the road, and some
are intent upon many evil deeds and some
on much good as they go both to and fro. To know
each one is difficult. But all day long until
the setting of the sun I dug about the slope
of my vineyard plot, and I thought, sir, but do not know
for certain, that I noticed a child, whoever he was,
who followed along behind the beautifully horned kine,
an infant. He had a staff and stepped from side to side
and drove them backward, their heads opposite him."
So the old man spoke, and Apollo, hearing his tale,
went more quickly on his way, and when he saw
a long-winged bird, straightway he knew that the robber was
the son of Kronian Zeus. The lord Apollo, son
of Zeus, leapt up and sped to very holy Pytho
in pursuit of his shambling-gaited cows, his broad back

clad in a crimson cloud. When the Far-archer spied
the cattle's tracks, he spoke and made a speech like this:
"Ho, ho, a mighty marvel is this that my eyes
behold! These are the tracks of my straight-horned cows,
but they are turned back to the meadow of asphodel.
But these are the footprints of neither woman nor man
nor of gray wolves or lions or bears, nor do I suppose
that they belong to a centaur of shaggy mane, who
with his swift feet makes monstrous tracks like these. Dire
are those this side of the road, more dire those on that."
Speaking so, the lord Apollo, son of Zeus,
sped and came to Kyllene's forest-clad mount
and deep-shadowed hollow of rock where the ambrosial nymph
gave birth to Hermes, the child of Zeus, the son of Kronos.
A lovely fragrance spread over the heavenly hill
where many long-shanked sheep were grazing the grass.
Hastening there the Far-archer Apollo himself
stepped over the stony threshold into the misty cave.
Now when the son of Zeus and Maia saw him,
the Far-archer, enraged about his stalwart cows,
he snuggled down inside his fragrant swaddling clothes,
as when the ash of wood covers the deep embers
of tree stumps, so Hermes, seeing the Far-archer,
cuddled himself up and huddled together his head
and feet in a little space like a freshly bathed child
seeking sweet sleep, though in truth wide awake,
and he kept his tortoiseshell lyre beneath the pit of his arm.
But the son of Zeus and Leto noticed and recognized
the very lovely mountain nymph and her dear son,
though a little child and swathed so cunningly.
Peering in every nook and niche of the big house,
and taking a shining key, he opened up three
cupboards full of nectar and lovely ambrosia. There lay
within a plentitude of silver and gold as well
as many crimson and silvery-colored clothes of the nymph,
such as the sacred homes of the blessed gods contain.
Then when the son of Leto had searched out the niches
and nooks of the great house, he spoke to glorious Hermes:
"O child, who lie in your cradle, tell me quickly about

255–293 my cows, since swiftly we two will quarrel indecently,
for I will hurl you into murky Tartaros,
to doom-ridden, irresistible gloom, and neither your mother
nor your father will release you to the light,
but beneath the earth you will roam, a leader to little men."
Then Hermes answered him with cunning words and said,
"Son of Leto, what harsh word is this that you
have uttered? Seeking rustic cows have you come here?
I have not seen nor heard of them from anyone.
I could not inform, nor could I take an informer's reward,
nor am I like a stalwart fellow, a cattle thief.
This is not my work. I have other concerns.
I care for sleep and my mother's milk and swaddling clothes
about my shoulders and warm baths. Let no one learn
this quarrel's cause. A mighty wonder it would be
among immortal gods if a newborn child should pass
through the forecourt with rustic cows. You speak absurdly.
Only yesterday was I born. My feet are soft,
and the earth beneath is rough. But if you wish, upon
my father's head I will swear a mighty oath and vow
that neither am I myself to blame nor have I seen
another thief of your cows, whatever cows may be.
For cows are something I know only by report."
So then he spoke. Sparking quick glances from
his eyes, he'd raise his brows, looking here and there,
and whistling long as if listening to a silly tale.
Laughing softly, the Far-archer Apollo said,
"You rascal, you trickster, you cunning rogue, I certainly think
that you have many times plundered well-built homes
this night and sat not one mortal alone upon
the floor, noiselessly cleaning him out throughout the house,
so cleverly you talk. Many a rustic shepherd
you'll vex in mountain glens, whenever, craving flesh,
you come upon the herds and thick-fleeced sheep.
But come, that this not be your last and final sleep,
climb out of your cradle, you companion of black night.
This honor will after be yours among the immortal gods:
you will be called the prince of robbers for all your days."
So Phoibos Apollo spoke and lifted and carried the child.

But then the strong Argeïphontes made his plan
and, carried in Phoibos' hands, he sent forth an omen,
his belly's hard-pressed effort, a reckless messenger,
and immediately after that he sneezed, and Apollo
heard and cast glorious Hermes to the ground
and sat before him, eager though he was for the road,
and, taunting Hermes, he spoke to him and said this word:
"Never mind, swaddling child of Zeus and Maia:
I shall find by these omens soon my heads of stalwart cattle,
and you yourself just now will lead me on my way."
So he spoke. Kyllenian Hermes leapt up
in eager haste. He shoved to his ears with both his hands
the swaddling clothes that wrapped his shoulders and said to him,
"Far-archer, where do you carry me, angriest
of all the gods? Is it because of your cows you are
so enraged and torment me like this? Dear me, if only
all cattle would die, for it was not I who stole your cows,
nor did I see another, whatever cows may be,
for I know them only by report. But let us go
to court and put the case to Zeus, Kronos' son."
So then the shepherd Hermes and Leto's glorious son
kept arguing explicitly every single thing,
each of them stubbornly. Apollo truthfully said
not wrongfully because of the cows had he tried to seize
glorious Hermes, but the Kyllenian god with tricks
and crafty words had hoped to deceive the Silver-bowed,
but when, wily though he was, he discovered him
resourceful too, he walked ahead across the sand,
with the son of Leto and Zeus behind. Soon they arrived
at the summit of fragrant Olympos and into the presence of
their father Kronian Zeus—those very lovely children—
and there were set for them both in that place the scales of Justice.
There was an assembly upon snowy Olympos, and there
were gathered the imperishable gods after the golden-throned
Dawn. Apollo of silver bow and Hermes stood
before the knees of Zeus, and Zeus who thunders on high
questioned his shining son and spoke this word to him:
"Phoibos, from where do you come, driving this mighty spoil,

331–372 a newborn child with the look of a herald. A serious thing
is this that has come before the gathering of the gods."
The Far-archer Apollo answered him in turn,
"O father, soon you will hear no trifling tale, although
you taunt me that I alone am a lover of spoil.
This child I found, a burgling thief, in Kyllene's hills
when I had covered much ground, a mocker such
as I have never seen among gods or men,
as many robbers as there may be upon the earth.
He stole from the meadow my cows and went driving them off
at evening along the shore of the loud-roaring sea and made
straight for Pylos. Monstrous and double were the tracks—
of a sort to marvel at, the work of an awesome god.
The dark dust kept and revealed the tracks of the cows
that led to the meadow of asphodel, but he himself,
perplexingly, with neither hands nor feet crossed
the sandy ground, but with some other device he tracked—
what a wondrous thing!—as though one walked upon
slender oaks. Now while he followed through sandy ground,
all the tracks were very obvious in the dust,
but after he had completed the great trek through the sand,
there suddenly disappeared the cows' tracks and his own
on the hard ground. But a mortal man took note of him
as he drove straight for Pylos the wide-browed cows.
But when he had penned them up in peace, he juggled his path
this way and that and lay in his cradle like black night
in the murk of the misty cave, nor would an eagle, keen
of sight, have spied him there. With his hands he'd rub his eyes,
contriving trickery, and bluntly he spoke straightway:
'I have not seen nor heard of them from anyone,
and so I could not inform nor take an informer's reward.'"
Speaking so, Phoibos Apollo sat down.
Hermes in turn addressed the immortal gods and said,
pointing to Kronos' son, commander of all the gods:
"Father Zeus, indeed I will tell the truth to you,
for I am truthful and know not how to tell a lie.
He came to our house to find his shambling-gaited cows,
today, just as the sun began to rise, but brought
of the blessed gods no witnesses or spies but bade

me confess with mighty violence and threatened again
and again to hurl me down to broad Tartaros,
for he has the tender bloom of glory-loving youth,
but I was born but yesterday, as he well knows.
Nor am I like a stalwart robber-man of cows.
Believe me, for you claim to be my father dear,
I did not drive the cattle home—so may I
be blessed!—nor step above the threshold. I tell the truth.
Helios I respect and the other gods and you
I love and him I dread. You know yourself that I
am not to blame. I will swear a mighty oath to it.
No, by these porticoes of the gods, richly adorned!
In time I'll punish him for pitiless detection,
powerful though he be. But help the younger ones."
  So Kyllenian Argeïphontes spoke with a wink
and kept his swaddling clothes upon his arms, nor cast
them aside, and Zeus laughed out loud at the mischievous child
cleverly denying guilt about the cows
and bade them both agree to seek the cattle and Hermes
the guide to lead the way and with innocence of mind
to show the spot where he had hid the stalwart cows.
The son of Kronos nodded and glorious Hermes obeyed,
for easily did the will of aegis-bearing Zeus
prevail. The two exceedingly beautiful children of Zeus
sped to sandy Pylos and came to Alpheus' ford
and reached the fields and high-roofed fold where the flocks
were sheltered by night, and Hermes went to the rocky cave
and started to drive to the light of day the stalwart cows.
The son of Leto, looking askance, observed the hides
of cows upon the sun-scorched rock and immediately asked,
  "How were you able, you crafty rascal, to flay two cows,
a newborn infant like you? I myself at least
marvel at the strength that will be yours. No need
to go on growing much, Kyllenian Maia's son."
  He spoke and twisted with his hands mighty bonds

. . . .

From the ground beneath their feet they sprouted at once, right there,

411–447 and, intricately entwined, they covered easily
all the rustic cattle by robber Hermes' plot.
Apollo was astonished at what he saw, and then
mighty Argeïphontes, flashing fire from his eyes,
glanced askance at the ground, and anxious to conceal

. . . .

But Hermes easily soothed the Far-archer, son
of very glorious Leto, as he himself wished,
strong as Apollo was. Upon his left arm
he lifted his lyre and with his key tried each string.
It sounded wondrously, and Phoibos Apollo laughed,
delightedly, for the lovely throb of the heavenly note
went to his heart, and a sweet longing seized his soul
as he heard. Playing beautifully upon his lyre,
the son of Maia courageously stood at the left hand
of Phoibos Apollo, and soon, as he harped, sweet and shrill,
he sang along, and lovely was his following voice,
describing immortal gods and the black earth and how
they came at first to be and how each one got
his share. Mnemosyne first of gods he honored in song,
the Muses' mother, for she attracted Maia's son.
The glorious son of Zeus honored the deathless gods
according to age—how each was born—telling all
in order as he played the lyre upon his arm.
Irresistible longing took hold of Apollo's heart in his breast,
and he spoke to Hermes and uttered winged words and said,
"Ox slayer, trickster, busy companion of the feast,
worth fifty cows are the songs that you have sung, and I
believe that peacefully we'll come to agreement soon.
But come, tell me now, Maia's wily son,
have these marvelous accomplishments been yours from birth,
or did some immortal god or mortal man bestow
upon you the noble gift and teach you heavenly song?
For wondrous is this newly uttered sound I hear
which no one ever yet, I say, of men has known
or of the immortal gods who dwell upon Olympos—
apart from you, O robber son of Zeus and Maia.
What skill, what muse for hopeless sorrows, what path

is this? For truly together and present are these three
from which to choose: merriment, love, and sweet sleep.
For though I attend the Olympian Muses, whose love is the dance
and the shining path of song—the sonorous melody,
the enchanting shrill of flutes—still my heart did not
rejoice so much at that skill of young men's feasts as it does
at this. I marvel, son of Zeus, that you play your lyre
so beautifully. But since you know such glorious arts,
little though you are, sit down, my pet, and pay
respect to your elders' words. For now you shall have renown
among immortal gods, yourself and your mother too.
I will tell you truly: yes, by this cornel-wood javelin,
I will make you a leader, illustrious and blessed among
the immortal gods and give you glorious gifts, nor
will I deceive you, either now or evermore."
    Hermes replied to him and spoke with cunning words:
"Far-archer, you question me with circumspection. But I
begrudge you not at all encroachment upon my art.
You shall know it today. I wish to be kind in counsel
and word, for you know all in your heart, for you sit first,
O son of Zeus, among the immortal gods, and you are brave
and strong, and Zeus in all his wisdom loves you,
with every right, and has given to you glorious gifts.
They say that honors you have learned from the voice of Zeus
and oracles too, Far-archer, from Zeus, and all his decrees.
Now of these I myself have learned [that you
have wealth]. Your choice it is to learn whatever you please,
but since it is your heart's desire to play the lyre,
sing and play, and making merriment, accept
this gift from me. Do you, my friend, give glory to me.
Sing well with this shrill-voiced friend in your hands, for you
understand lovely and beautifully ordered utterance.
With assurance afterward bring it to the bounteous feast,
the lovely dance, and glorious revel, merriment
by night and day. Whoever with art and skill inquires
of it and learns, sounded, it teaches every kind
of thing that charms the mind when easily played and with
accustomed delicacy, avoiding drudgery.
But whoever, unskilled, inquires of it with violence,

for him it sounds false with foolish nonsense and vain.
But I will give you this lyre, glorious son of Zeus,
I myself, Far-archer, with rustic cattle will graze
the pastures of hill and horse-rearing plain, and so cows
covered by bulls will bear sufficiently both males
and females. Nor is there any need for you to be
cunning, though you are angered outrageously."

Speaking so, he offered and Phoibos Apollo accepted
the lyre and put the shining whip in Hermes' hand
and gave him command of herds. The son of Maia accepted
delightedly. Taking upon his left arm
the lyre, Leto's glorious son, the Far-archer, lord Apollo
tried each string with the key and at his touch it sounded
wondrously, and beautifully the god sang.

And then from there they turned the cattle back again
to the holy meadows, and they themselves, the very lovely
children of Zeus, sped back once more to snowy Olympos,
taking delight in the lyre, and Zeus in his wisdom rejoiced
and brought them both together as friends, and Hermes loved
the son of Leto continuously, as even now,
once he had put as token into the Far-archer's hands
the lovely lyre and Apollo played it skillfully,
balancing it upon his arm. Hermes himself
found out the art of another skill and made for himself
the sound of the shepherd's pipes which are heard from far away,
and then the son of Leto spoke to Hermes and said,

"Son of Maia, wily-minded messenger,
I fear lest you steal from me my lyre and my bent bow,
for you have from Zeus the office of establishment
of bartering for men throughout the fertile earth.
But if you would agree to swear the mighty oath
of gods, either by nodding your head or by the Styx's
potent water, you would do all to please my heart."

Then the son of Maia promised, nodding his head,
never to steal anything Far-archer possessed
nor to approach his well-built house. And Leto's son,
Apollo, vowed in bond of friendship and love that none
among the immortal gods would be more dear to him,
neither god nor human offspring of Zeus, complete

. . . .

"I will make you a symbol for all the immortal gods alike, 527–564
honored and trusted by my heart. And afterward
I will give you of riches and wealth a very beautiful staff,
three-leafed and gold. It will keep you unharmed as you fulfill
every command of word or deed, those that are good,
that I profess to know through Zeus' utterance.
Prophecy, O noblest, divinely cherished child,
of which you ask, by law you may not learn nor may
the other immortal gods. Only the mind of Zeus
knows this. But I have pledged and nodded to and sworn
a powerful oath that no one apart from me of all
the eternal gods shall know the sapient counsel of Zeus.
Do not, my brother of golden staff, bid me reveal
the ordinances that wide-seeing Zeus contrives.
One of men I will damage, another benefit,
perplexing many tribes of melancholy men.
Through my utterance there shall be without pain
the man who comes by voice and flight of prophetic birds,
nor will I deceive him. But whoever, putting his trust
in foolishly chirping birds, comes to inquire against
my will of my prophetic art and to know more
than the ever-living gods comes, I say, upon
a useless path. But still I would accept his gifts.
And I will tell you something else as well, O son
of very glorious Maia and aegis-bearing Zeus,
luck-bringing sprite of the gods. There are certain holy ones,
sisters born, virgins that glory in swift wings—
three—whose heads are sprinkled with white barley meal.
They dwell beneath a fold of Mount Parnassos. Apart
from the mantic art I practiced while still a little child
tending cows, they teach the art of prophecy.
My father paid no heed. Flying then from there,
now this way, now that, they feed on honeycomb and make
everything come to pass. Inspired by feeding upon
the pale honey, they are eager to tell the truth.
But if they are deprived of the gods' sweet repast,
they lie, and then they swarm about among one another.
These I give to you. Ask of them precisely.

565–580 Delight your heart. And if you teach a mortal man,
often he'll hear your utterance—if he has luck.
Take these, O son of Maia, and tend the rustic cows
of crumpled horns, the horses, and patient hard-working mules."

. . . .

gleaming-eyed lions and boars with flashing tusks
and dogs and all the flocks the broad earth nourishes
and all sheep glorious Hermes was to rule
and be alone appointed messenger to Hades,
who although he takes no gift will give not
the least of prizes. So the lord Apollo loved
Hermes, the son of Maia, with every kind of affection
and Kronos' son bestowed upon him grace as well.
With all immortals and mortals too does he consort.
He helps them a little but throughout the dark night
deceives unceasingly the tribes of mortal men.
    So now farewell to you, son of Zeus and Maia.
But I will remember you and also another song.

V

Hymn to Aphrodite

Speak to me, Muse, of the deeds of golden Aphrodite,
the Kyprian, who stirs in gods sweet desire
and masters the tribes of mortal men, the birds that fly,
and all the wild beasts the dry land feeds and the sea.
All delight in Kythereia, beautifully crowned.
But three are the hearts that she can neither persuade nor beguile:
the first is that of the daughter of aegis-bearing Zeus,
gleaming-eyed Athena. Golden Aphrodite's
enchantments gave no pleasure to her, but wars and the work
of Ares, combats and battles and preparation of
glorious crafts delighted her, for she first taught
earthly artisans to fashion chariots of war
and cars intricately wrought of bronze, and she
taught virgin girls of tender flesh within the house
glorious arts, instilling skill in the mind of each.
Nor does laughter-loving Aphrodite subdue
in love huntress Artemis of golden shaft,
for she delights in bows and slaying of beasts on hills
and dances and lyres and piercing cries and shadowy groves
and cities of just men. Nor does the revered maid,
Hestia, delight in Aphrodite's deeds,
whom Kronos of crooked counsel first begat. She was
the youngest too, by will of aegis-bearing Zeus,
a queen to whom Apollo and Poseidon paid court,
but she was most unwilling and stubbornly declined.
She swore a mighty oath, accomplished since, and touched
the head of the father, aegis-bearing Zeus, that she,
shining of goddesses, would be a virgin all
her days, and father Zeus gave to her in place
of wedlock lovely honor. She sits amid the house
and has the choicest lot. In all the temples of gods
she has her honor. Among all mortal men she is
the most respected of goddesses. Of these three

33–71 Aphrodite cannot persuade nor beguile the hearts.
But of all others nothing at all of the blessed gods
or of mortal men has escaped Aphrodite. Even the mind
of Zeus who delights in thunder has she seduced, though he
is mightiest and has of honor the mightiest share.
Even his shrewd wits she beguiles easily
whenever she pleases and mates him with mortals, when she
can escape the notice of Hera, his sister and wedded wife,
who is the most beautiful by far among
immortal goddesses, most glorious too, whom
Kronos of crooked counsel begat with Rhea her mother.
Zeus of imperishable wisdom made her his bride,
his chastely wedded and properly prudent and gracious wife.
    But in the soul of Aphrodite herself Zeus
instilled sweet desire to lie with a mortal man
that very soon she not herself be innocent
of a mortal bed and someday boast and say among
all the gods, smiling sweetly, Aphrodite,
the laughter-loving, that she had mated immortal gods
to mortal women who bore to deathless gods sons
of death and mated goddesses to mortal men.
    For Anchises then he instilled in her soul sweet desire,
who then on the lofty hills of many-fountained Ida
was pasturing cows, and he was like immortals to see.
At sight of him laughter-loving Aphrodite
fell in love. Desire seized violently at her heart.
To Kypros, to Paphos she went and entered her fragrant shrine.
There her precinct is and her fragrant altars too.
Going inside, she put to the gleaming doors,
and the Graces bathed and anointed her with ambrosial oil
such as blossoms upon the limbs of eternal gods,
deliciously ambrosial and fragrant beside her.
Putting about her flesh all her lovely clothes,
gold-bedecked, laughter-loving Aphrodite
hastened to Troy, abandoning sweetly scented Kypros,
nimbly taking her path high among the clouds.
She came to many-fountained Ida, mother of beasts,
and went straight to the steading across the mountain. After her
fawning gray wolves and bright-eyed lions came

and bears and leopards, swift and insatiable of deer.
Seeing them she rejoiced in her heart and cast in their breasts
desire, and so they all, two by two, took mates
throughout the shadowy vales. She herself arrived
at the well-built shelters and found him left alone, apart
from others, Anchises, the hero, who had the beauty of gods.
All the others followed cattle through grassy pastures,
but he, left in the steadings alone, apart from the rest,
wandered here and there, playing piercingly
upon his lyre. Before him there stood the daughter of Zeus,
Aphrodite, like a virgin girl in appearance and height
lest he take fright at sight of her. When Anchises saw,
he took note and marveled at her appearance and height
and glittering clothes, for she wore a robe more dazzling than fire
and twisted bracelets and earrings like gleaming buds
and around her delicate throat lovely necklaces,
gorgeous, gold, and intricately wrought. Like the moon
they shone upon her tender breasts, a wonder to see.
Anchises was seized with love and spoke opposite her:
    "Greetings, queen, whoever you are of the blessed who come
to this house, Artemis, Leto, or golden Aphrodite,
or Themis, wellborn, or gleaming-eyed Athena or
perhaps as one of the Graces you've come here, who are
companions to all the gods and are called immortal, or one
of the nymphs who haunt these lovely groves, this beautiful hill,
and the springs of rivers and grassy meadows. For you I'll build
on a mountain peak, a conspicuous place, an altar and make
lovely sacrifices in every season. And do you
with kindly heart grant that I become among
the Trojans a most distinguished man and make my stock
flourishing in aftertime and that I myself
live well and long and look upon the light of the sun
and come, among my people blessed, to the threshold of age."
    Then Aphrodite, the daughter of Zeus, answered him:
"Anchises, most glorious of men born on earth,
no goddess am I. Why do you compare me to
immortal gods? Mortal am I, of a woman born.
Otreus is my father, famous of name. You have
heard of him perhaps. He rules all of Phrygia,

113–151 beautifully walled. I know your tongue as well as mine,
for a Trojan nurse reared me in our house, for she
took me from my mother, still a little child,
and cherished me. And so I know your tongue well.
But now Argeïphontes of golden wand has snatched
me up from the dance of huntress Artemis who has
the golden shaft. We many nymphs and richly courted
maids were playing, encircled by a countless crowd.
From them Argeïphontes of golden wand snatched
me away and carried me over many plowed fields
of mortal men and much land, untilled, unowned,
where carnivorous wild beasts roam through shadowy groves,
nor did I expect to touch with my feet the life-giving earth.
He said that I'd be called Anchises' wedded wife
and would bear glorious children to you. But when
he had shown and told all this, mighty Argeïphontes
went away again to the tribes of immortal gods.
But I have come to you, for strong necessity
compels me. By Zeus and your noble parents—for base ones
could not produce a son like you—I beseech you:
take me, a virgin, innocent of love, and show
me to your father, your prudent mother, and your brothers
who are born of the same stock. To them I shall not be
an unseemly daughter-in-law, but rather a seemly one.
Swiftly send a messenger to the fleet-horsed Phrygians
to tell my father, and mother who grieves, and they will send
to you gold in plenty and garments of woven work.
Accept these many glorious gifts as price for a bride.
Do this and then prepare the lovely wedding feast
that finds honor among both men and immortal gods."
    Speaking so, the goddess cast sweet desire
in his soul, and Anchises spoke this word and called her by name:
    "If you are mortal, and if a woman bore you,
and Otreus is your father, famous of name, as you say,
and if by the will of Hermes, the deathless messenger,
you have come here to be called my wife for all your days,
then no one of gods or mortal men shall keep me
from lying in love with you right now, immediately,
not even if Far-archer Apollo himself should shoot

wounding shafts from his silver bow. I'd be willing then, O woman who are as lovely as the goddesses, to go down to Hades' house once I'd gone up to your bed." *152–186*

So he spoke and took her hand, and laughter-loving Aphrodite turned aside, her lovely eyes downcast, and crept to the bed, beautifully spread, which had even before been strewn with luxurious coverlets. Upon it lay the skins of bears and deep-roaring lions which Anchises himself had slain on the lofty mountaintops. And when they had mounted the beautifully crafted bed, then first he took from her flesh her glittering jewelry, her brooches and twisted bracelets, her petal earrings, her necklaces. He loosed her sash and then took off her gleaming garments and put them, Anchises did, upon a silver-studded chair, and then by the gods' will and destiny he lay, a mortal man, in love with an immortal goddess, not knowing what he did.

When herdsmen drive back to the fold their cattle and fat sheep from flowering fields, then Aphrodite shed upon Anchises delightful sweet sleep, but she herself put on her lovely clothes. And when the shining one of goddesses had dressed herself completely and well, then she stood beside the bed and her head reached the properly fitted roof beam. The ambrosial beauty of her cheeks shone round about and it was like the glow that belongs to beautifully garlanded Kythereia. She roused him from sleep and spoke this word and called him by name:

"Son of Dardanos, arise. Why do you sleep so deeply? Consider if I appear exactly as I did when first you took note of me with your eyes."

So she spoke, and he awoke from his sleep and obeyed, readily. When he saw the neck and lovely eyes of Aphrodite, he was afraid and turned his eyes elsewhere, aside, and hid his handsome face in his cloak, and then, beseeching her, he uttered winged words:

"Immediately, as soon as I saw you first, I knew that you were a goddess. You did not speak truthfully.

187–223 But you I beseech by aegis-bearing Zeus, do not
leave me to live enfeebled with men but pity me,
since he who lies in love with immortal goddesses
can never after become a hale and hearty man."

And then Aphrodite, the daughter of Zeus, replied to him:
"Courage, Anchises, most honored of mortal men. Do not
fear overmuch in your heart. You need not be afraid
of evil from me nor from the rest of the blessed, for you
are dear to the gods, and you shall have a dear son
who shall reign among the Trojans and children from his children,
born successively. His name shall be Aineias,
because I grieved terribly that I yielded to
the bed of a mortal man. Always especially like
the gods are those from your stock of mortal men in both
beauty and stature of form. Indeed, sagacious Zeus
because of his beauty snatched up blond Ganymede
to be among the deathless gods and in the house
of Zeus to pour out wine for the gods—a marvel to see—
honored by all immortal gods as he ladles out
from the krater of gold the rosy nectar. Incessant grief
seized the heart of Tros, nor did he know at all
where the divine whirlwind had rapt his dear son,
and afterward for all his days he mourned for him,
continuously, and Zeus pitied him and gave
to him as recompense for his son high-stepping steeds
of the sort that carry abroad immortal divinities.
These he gave as a gift to keep. And Argeïphontes,
the guide, at Zeus' behest told him everything,
how his son would be unaging and immortal, just like
the gods. When Tros heard the pronouncements of Zeus, he grieved
no more but rejoiced in his heart and rode his storm-footed steeds.

"So again did Dawn of the golden throne snatch
Tithonos, of your stock and like the immortal gods.
She went to ask the son of Kronos of black clouds
that he be immortal and live for all eternal days.
Zeus nodded assent to her and fulfilled her heart's desire.
Fool that she was, the lady Dawn did not think

to ask for youth, to slough off the skin of destructive age,
so while enchanting youth encompassed him, he rejoiced
to dwell with early-born Dawn of golden throne beside
the Ocean's floods at the limits of earth. But when the first
gray hairs appeared on his beautiful head and noble chin,
then the lady Dawn kept away from his bed,
though she kept and cherished him in her house and gave to him
ambrosia and bread and beautiful garments to wear. But when
loathsome old age had pressed completely upon him,
and he could not move nor lift his limbs, then this appeared
to her in her heart to be the noblest plan. She laid
Tithonos in a room and shut the shining doors.
There he babbles senselessly, nor has he the strength
that once he had in his pliant limbs. Not such as this
would I have you be deathless among the deathless gods
and live forevermore. But if, such as you are,
in beauty and form, you could live on and be called my spouse,
then afterward grief would not enshroud my prudent heart.
But as it is, a like old age will soon enshroud
you too, pitilessly, such as befalls men,
destructive, exhausting, loathsome to even the gods. But now
I shall have great shame among the immortal gods because
of you, continuously, forevermore. Before
they feared my dalliance and plots by which once
I mated to mortal women all the immortal gods,
for my intent subdued them all. No longer now
will my mouth contain the power to call by name this right
among the immortals, for I was most infatuate,
and very wickedly, and wandering from my wits,
I put a babe beneath my sash from a mortal's bed.
    "When first that child beholds the light of the sun, then
the full-breasted mountain nymphs will nourish him. They dwell
upon this mighty and very sacred mountain, and they
attend neither mortal men nor immortal gods.
Long do they live and eat ambrosial food and with
immortal gods they dance in lovely choruses.
With them the Silenoi and keen-sighted Argeïphontes
mingle in love in the uttermost depths of lovely caves,
and at their birth pines and oaks of lofty tops

265–293 spring up upon the fertile earth, beautiful,
flourishing long upon the lofty mountaintops,
and towering high. They are called the sacred precincts of
immortal gods, nor do mortals lop them with
the iron ax. But when the lot of death stands near,
first upon the earth the lovely trees are parched,
the bark shrivels about them and twigs fall
and the souls of both abandon together the light of the sun.
These goddesses will keep and nourish with them my son.
When first he reaches the lovely blossom of youth, they will bring
him here to you and show you your child. That I may tell
to you all that I have in mind, toward the fifth year
I shall come again and bring my son. When first you see
with your eyes this shoot, you'll rejoice at the sight, for he will be
exceedingly like a god. You will take him straightway
to windy Ilion. If any mortal man
shall ask what mother put your son beneath her sash,
remember to reply exactly as I bid:
they say that he is the sprig of the budded-blossoming nymphs
who inhabit this forest-clad hill. But if you speak out and boast
with thoughtless heart that you lay in love with Kythereia,
beautifully crowned, Zeus in his rage will smite you with
a smoking thunderbolt. Now all is said. Pay heed,
refrain, name me not, respect the god's wrath."
    So she spoke and darted up to windy heaven.
    Goddess, farewell, who rule Kypros, beautifully built.
I began with you. I'll change now to another song.

VI

Hymn to Aphrodite

Of venerable Aphrodite, golden garlanded
and lovely, will I sing, whose lot is battlemented
Kypros upon the sea. There the moist breath
of the West Wind bore her over the wave of the loud-
roaring sea in soft foam. The Hours who wear
the golden diadems welcomed her delightedly
and clothed her in ambrosial robes and placed upon
her immortal head a lovely crown, well wrought, of gold.
In her pierced ears they put rings of precious gold
and orichalc and about her tender neck and upon
her snowy breasts they adorned her with golden necklaces
which the Hours themselves, golden diademed, wear whenever
they go to the lovely choruses of the gods and to
their father's house. When they had ornamented her,
they brought her to the deathless gods, who welcomed her,
extending hands at the sight of her, and each one prayed
that he lead her home his wedded wife, marveling at
the wondrous beauty of Kythereia, the violet crowned.
Farewell, O sweetly beguiling, glancing-eyed. Grant
that in this contest I win the prize. Command my song.
I shall remember you and another song as well.

VII

Hymn to Dionysos

About Dionysos, son of glorious Semele,
I will tell, how he appeared upon the thrust
of the cape at the shore of the barren sea like a young man
in the first flower of youth. His lovely blue-black locks
shook about and on his sturdy shoulders he wore
a crimson cloak. Soon men from a well-benched ship arrived
with speed upon the sparkling wine-bright sea. They were
pirates from Tyrsenia. An evil doom
led them on. Spying him, they gave the nod
and quickly leapt out and straightway seized and cast him aboard
their ship, rejoicing in their hearts, for they thought him to be
the son of divinely nurtured kings. With galling bonds
they sought to fetter him, but him the bonds would not
contain, and the shackles fell far from his hands and feet.
He sat with a smile in his blue-black eyes. The pilot straightway
understood and called to his companions and said,
"Are you possessed? What god is this that you seize and bind,
mighty that he is? Not even a well-wrought ship
can carry him. Surely this is Zeus, or Apollo
of the silver bow, or Poseidon, for not like mortal men
is he to see but the gods who have Olympian homes.
But let us abandon him upon the black shore
straightway nor lay our hands upon him, lest he in anger
arouse dangerous winds and mighty hurricanes."
So he spoke. But the captain rebuked him with scolding words:
"Madman, watch the wind and help to hoist the sail,
holding all the sheets. We men will handle him.
I expect he's bound for Egypt or for Kypros or
the Hyperboreans or further beyond. But in the end
he will speak forth his friends and all that he possesses,
his brothers too, since fortune tosses him to us."
Speaking so, he had mast and sail hoist

upon the ship. The wind bellied the sail, and they drew
taut the sheets on either side. But soon there appeared
among them wondrous works. First a fragrant wine,
sweet to the taste, burbled throughout the swift black ship,
and there arose an ambrosial aroma. Amazement embraced
all the sailors who saw. Straightway there spread upon
the top of the sail, on this side and that, a vine, and there hung
down from it many clusters of grapes. About the mast
there twined a dark ivy, flourishing with buds,
and exquisite fruit blossomed upon it, and all the tholes
wore garlands. Seeing this, the pirates bade the pilot
put the ship to shore. Within the ship the god
became at the bow a terrible lion and roared loud.
Amidship he made a shaggy bear, revealing his signs.
It reared and raged. At the peak of the deck the lion scowled,
dreadfully. The sailors fled in fright to the stern,
and, terrified, they crowded about the prudent pilot.
Suddenly the lion sprang and seized the captain.
Escaping evil doom, all the sailors leapt,
when they saw, overboard, into the sparkling sea,
and they became dolphins. In pity for the pilot,
Dionysos held him back and made him blessed and said,
"Courage . . . for you have delighted my heart.
I am Dionysos who roars loud and whom
my mother bore, Kadmos' daughter Semele,
when she had lain in love in the bed of father Zeus."
Farewell, O child of Semele of the lovely face.
No one forgetful of you can command a sweet song.

XXVIII

Hymn to Athena

Pallas Athena, the glorious goddess, I begin to sing,
gray-eyed, of many wiles, implacable
of heart, a modest virgin, protector of fortresses,
courageous, Tritogeneia, to whom sagacious Zeus
himself gave birth from his august head, bedecked
in martial arms flashing gold. All the gods
were seized with awe as they beheld, but she arose,
violently, from his immortal head, and stood
before Zeus of the aegis, and shook a sharp spear.
Mighty Olympos trembled terribly before
the strength of the gray-eyed one, and the earth around cried
horribly, and the sea was stirred and billowed high
with purple-black waves and suddenly foamed with brine.
The brilliant son of Hyperion stayed his fleet-foot steeds
a long while, until Pallas Athena had stripped
from her immortal shoulders the godlike weaponry,
and Zeus, wise in all his counsels, rejoiced and was glad.
And so farewell, daughter of aegis-bearing Zeus.
I shall remember you and another song as well.

ARCHILOCHOS

I

I am the squire of lord Enyalios,
but I know too the Muses' lovely gift.

2

By the spear my bread is kneaded. With the spear I win
my Ismarian wine, which I drink while I lean on my spear.

3

Not many will be the bows stretched nor frequent the slings
    when Ares conducts his battle brawl to the plain,
but then the struggle of swords will make many a moan,
    for in battle like this those are devilishly skilled,
the lords of Euboia, famed for mastery with the spear.

4

But come with the cup along the thwarts of the swift ship
    and draw drink from the hollow tubs
and drain the red wine to the dregs. No more can we
    than other men be sober on this watch.

5

Some Saian now delights in my shield which I left behind,
    despite myself, beside a bush—no fault
of it—but I saved my skin. What's that shield to me?
    Let it go! I'll get me another no worse.

6

favoring the foe with guest-gifts of woe

8

Many times in the gray brine
of the fair-haired sea
we begged for sweet return.

9.10–11

If Hephaistos had attended to his head
    and lovely limbs in shining dress

11

I'll cure nothing by weeping, nor will I make it worse
    by pursuit of joy and cheerful festivity.

12

Let us conceal the grievous gifts of Lord Poseidon.

13

No citizen in reproach of heartbreaking sorrow, nor
    city, Perikles, will take joy
in the feast: Such were those that the wave of the roaring sea
    submerged, and we have hearts swollen with grief.
But for incurable woes the gods, my friend, have bestowed
    as a drug stalwart endurance. One man now,
another then, suffers such. It's our turn now,
    and we bewail a bloody wound. In time
others will have their turn. As soon as you possibly can,
    thrust aside this womanly grief and endure.

15

A mercenary's your friend, Glaukos,
for just so long as he fights for you.

18

son of Ares, stained with blood

19

I don't care about Gyges and all his gold.
I'm not jealous of him. I don't envy
the deeds of the gods nor long for rule.
These things are all far from my eyes.

20

I weep for the woes of Thasos
and not for Magnesia's woes.

21

Like the backbone of an ass
this island bristles
with wild brush.

22

For there is no country so fair
or lovely or desirable
as that where the Siris flows.

23

"Woman, be not distressed at this evil report
from men. For the kindly will be my concern, so be

of gracious intent. Do I seem to have come to such
a depth of wretchedness? Of cowardice?
Not such am I nor born from such, but this
I understand: how to love him
who loves me and hate my enemy.
I am an Ant. There's truth in that report.
This city . . . that you stroll
men have never sacked before, but you
have taken it with spear and won renown.
Be queen of it and wield a tyranny,
and you will be the envy of many men."

25.2

Different things warm different hearts.

26.5–6

Lord Apollo, reveal the guilty.
Destroy them as you always do.

30 and 31

She rejoiced in the spray of myrtle
she held and in the lovely bloom
of the rose. Her hair was a shadow
that fell down her shoulders and back.

34

Without a wage we'll never ferry you.

35

We have a haughty plow ox.
He knows how to work but won't.

36

They leaned against the wall in the shadowy dark.

38

Lykambes' younger daughter alone

41

flapped her wings
like the halcyon
on a beetling rock

42

The way a man from Phrygia
or Thrace sucks down his ale
with a straw, just so did she,
crouched, suck him off.

43

His penis swelled
like that of a he-
ass from Priene
gobbling the grain.

45

Hanging their heads, they sputtered out
all their bullying at once.

46

out of the pipe
and into the pail

48.5–6

They anointed their hair and their breasts
with myrrh so that even an old man
would have been enamored of them.

67.3

For I know another good cure
for a cancerous growth like this.

88

Erxias, where does this hapless host assemble?

91

May the stone of Tantalos
not hang over this isle.

93a

Men that played the flute and lyre he led
to Thasos, bringing as gifts for Thracian dogs
unadulterated gold, and there
for private gain they wrought public harm.

101

Of the seven dead whom we overtook on foot
we are the thousand slayers.

102

How the grief of all the Greeks has come together in Thasos.

105

Look, Glaukos! The sea is running high. A cloud
stands on end over the Gyraian cape, a sign
of storm. Fear comes only from the unforeseen.

107

I hope that the Dog Star
will wither many of them
with his piercing rays.

108

Lord Hepaistos, hear and be
propitious ally to me as I
supplicate you, and favor me
with whatever favors you will.

109

O outcast fellow townsmen, understand my words.

111

Embolden the young. The bounds of victory lie with the gods.

114

I don't like a general that's straddling or tall
nor one half-shaven with pretty curls.
I want one crooked of shank and short,
stout in his stance and full of heart.

115

Now Leophilos rules. Leophilos
prevails. Leophilos has everything,
and so you'd better obey Leophilos now.

116

Farewell to Paros and those figs and the seafaring life.

117

Sing of Glaukos who wears his hair like a horn.

118

If I could but touch Neoboule's hand.

119

to fall upon the paunch
and work belly to belly,
thigh against thigh

120

I know how to lead the lovely dithyrambic song
of lord Dionysos, my wits thunderstruck with wine.

121

I myself to the tune of the flute
lead off the Lesbian paian song.

122

There is nothing beyond hope nor abjured
nor past belief since Olympian father Zeus
has made night from noon by hiding the light
of the shining sun and enfeebling fear came
upon men, and so everything now can be
expected or believed. Let no one of you
who sees be surprised if wild beasts
accept the dolphins' briny pasturage
and the echoing wave of the sea becomes more dear
than the land to those who loved the forested hills.

124

. . . drinking much and unmixed wine
with no contribution to cost . . .
nor were you invited as though a friend,
but you beguiled your wits and your mind
to shamelessness . . .

125

I long to battle with you
as when I thirst to drink.

126

One big thing I understand:
how to repay with evil reproach
the man who evilly does me wrong.

127

I sinned, and I suppose
this retribution has come
upon another too.

128

Soul, my soul, disturbed by irresistible woes,
rise up, ward the enemy off, thrusting your chest
against the ambush, and stand staunch against the foe,
and if you win, do not obviously exult,
nor beaten, fall upon your back and weep and wail at home.
Do not rejoice in what delights or at evils grieve
excessively, but know the rhythm possessing men.

129

It's because of your friends
that you strangle yourself.

130

Trust to the gods for everything,
for often they raise from their troubles men
who lie upon the black earth,
and often they toss flat on their backs
even those whose tread was secure.
Many the evils that follow then,
and a man wanders about in need
of livelihood and out of his mind.

131 and 132

Such becomes the soul of mortal man,
Glaukos, Leptines' son, as Zeus may bring
for the day. His thoughts will match the deeds that he meets.

133

No man, once he is dead, gets respect
or honor from his fellow citizens,
so let us rather pursue favor from
the living while we live. For always the dead
get the very worst of everything.

134

It doesn't do to mock the dead.

168

Charilaos, Erasmon's son, I'll tell
you something droll, dearest by far
of my companions, and you'll delight,
I swear, at the very telling of it.

172

Father Lykambes, what is this that you've thought?
    Who has unhinged the wits
with which you were fitted before? Now you appear
    a great big laugh to all.

173

You've turned your back
on a mighty oath
and table and salt.

174

This is a fable of men:
a fox and an eagle once
met and became friends.

176

Do you see that towering rock, rough
    and treacherous? There
I sit, scorning battle with you.

177

O Zeus, father Zeus, yours is heaven's force.
  You oversee the deeds of men,
villainous and lawful too, and you are concerned
  with behavior of beasts, both brutal and just.

178

Lest you meet the black-rumped one

179

A dismal feast he brought and placed before his sons.

180

A spark of fire was I to him.

182

When the people gathered for the games
and among them Batousiades . . .

184

In one hand this beguiling girl
carries water; and in the other flame.

185

I'll tell you a fable, O Herald's Son, like
  a perplexing messenger-stick:
the ape apart from the beasts was walking alone
  in the utter outback
when the cunning fox met up with him, and he had
  craftiness at heart.

186

propped on the trap-stick

187

Such a rump as you've got, O ape.

188

The blossom is gone from your luscious flesh.
It's withered to furrows now
of ugly old age . . . there wipes clean . . .
and from your lovely face
all loveliness is gone,
for many blasts of wintry winds
have often made assault . . .

189

Many a blind eel
have you received.

190

and rugged mountain glens,
such was he in his youth

191

Such was love's desire
that twisted beneath my heart,
misted over my eyes,
and stole the soft wits
from out of my breast.

193

I lie nearly dead with desire.
The gods have pierced my bones
with these bitter pangs.

194

Each man drank from dawn,
in Bacchic . . .

195

to take an obvious evil to wife

196

But oh, companion of mine,
desire that looses the limbs
completely masters me.

196a

"Altogether holding off . . .

If you are pressed and passion impels,
there is among us one
already filled with desire,

a lovely tender girl. I think
her beauty blameless. Now her
do you . . ."

So she spoke, and I replied,
"Daughter of Amphimedo,
that noble and perspicacious

woman, whom now the broad earth
embraces, many delights
the goddess provides young men

outside the sacred act. Of these
one will suffice. In peace
until the [day] grows dark

shall we with god deliberate.
I will do only as
you bid. Just to come

beneath the coping and through the gate.
Don't begrudge me this,
dear girl, for I shall stop

within your orchard grass. And know:
another man can have
Neoboule, overripe . . .

The blossom of her maidenhood
is gone, and her former charm.
Insatiate . . .

Her measure the raving woman shows.
Off with her to the crows!
And this [may heaven grant],

that I for having a woman like this
not be my neighbor's butt.
It's you I want instead!

For you are not deceitful or sly,
but she is very sharp
and makes many . . .

I'm afraid she'll bear pups blind
and premature, for she's
as eager for sex as a bitch."

So much I said and took the girl
and laid her among the blossoming
buds, covering her

with my soft cloak, cradling her neck
in my arms. She trembled with fear
like a delicate fawn . . .

Tenderly I touched her breasts
just where Hebe's touch
revealed her youthful flesh.

All her lovely body I stroked
and let go my white force
to touch her tawny hair.

197

Father Zeus, no wedding feast did I attend.

200

He'll not get off scot-free from me.

201

The fox knows many things, the hedgehog only one.
One big one.

205

An old woman, you shouldn't
anoint yourself with myrrh.

210

What divinity and furious with whom . . .

211

skilled with the three-pronged fishing spear
and clever as a steersman too

212

stood at the brim of wave and wind

216

A mercenary shall I be called,
exactly like a Carian.

217

Skin-close from his shoulders
is shorn his mane.

218

I come in quest of you
and so create an omen.

223

You've got a cricket by the wing.

224

cowering like a partridge

228

Thasos, the city thrice pitiable

234

for to your liver you have no gall

252

Burst are my member's tendons.

297

The loathsome babbler strolled the halls.

298

Zeus among the gods a prophet most without lies,
he himself holds all accomplishment.

325

The lofty pillars of Naxos you have upon you,
Aristophon and Megatimos, O mighty Earth.

326

Alkibia dedicated the sacred veil from her locks
when she became a lawfully wedded wife.

330

An idle life is fine for the old,
especially if they're simple in
their ways and probably stupid too,
babbling nonsense all the time
as old men usually do.

331

The fig tree on its rock feeds many crows.
Simpleminded Pasiphile takes all who come.

KALLINOS

How long will you in idleness lie? When will you show,
    O youths, stoutness of heart? Are you not
ashamed before the dwellers-about to be at ease,
    sitting in peace while all the land's at war?

. . . .

    Let a man as he dies cast his javelin
one last time. For honor and glory bedeck the man
    who fights for his land, his children, and wedded wife.
Death will come at whatever time with enemy men
    the Fates spin out. Let him go forward
with brandished spear and keeping clamped beneath his shield
    a stout heart once the war's begun.
No mortal can possibly escape his destined death,
    not even if he's born from immortal stock.
Escaping many times the battle clash and crash
    of javelins, death overtakes him at home.
Nevertheless, he's neither dear nor bewept by the folk,
    though the other's bemoaned when he dies by great and small;
for all the people long for the strong-hearted man when he dies,
    and while he lives he's like a demigod,
for in their sight he seems a towering battlement
    who does the deeds of many, though only one.

SEMONIDES

7

God fashioned at first woman apart from mind.
One he made from a hairy sow. Throughout
her house everything's smeared with mud and rolls
around in utter confusion upon the ground.
Unwashed herself, in filthy clothes she sits
upon the heaps of dung and grows fat.
    Another god made from a knavish female fox,
a vixen who's clever at everything. Nothing
gets by her, whether it's better or worse.
Often she calls the bad good and then
the reverse. Her temper changes all the time.
    Another from a busybody bitch,
just like her mother. She's got to hear all,
know every single thing. Peering about,
she snoops and barks if she sees no one at all.
You can't stop her with threats, not even if
in your rage you take a rock and knock out her teeth,
nor even if you speak sweetly to her,
nor if she sits among strangers and guests.
She'll still keep up her whining, pointlessly.
    Another the Olympians made of earth
and gave her, maimed of wit, to a man to keep.
She doesn't know a thing, whether better or worse
but understands only how to eat,
nor if god makes the winter hard, does she,
though shivering, draw her chair nearer the fire.
    Another from the sea. Her moods are two.
One day she smiles and laughs delightedly.
A stranger would praise the sight of her in the house:
"There's no better wife than this among mankind
nor lovelier." The next she's insufferable—
you can't look or come near. She's like a bitch

with pups. Nasty tempered, implacable,
the same to friends and enemies, and as
the sea will often stand without a ripple
or threat, to sailors an enormous delight,
in summertime, but then with maddened rage
will billow and crash with loud thundering waves,
exactly such in disposition's a wife
like this, nor does the ocean's temper differ.

Another from a stolid donkey that's cudgeled
much. She works only when she's forced
or with threats, and never finishes anything.
Meanwhile she sits in the corner and eats, all day,
all night, and when it comes to sex, she takes
to her bed whomever she wants who comes along.

Another from a weasel, a miserable breed.
For her there's nothing at all that's lovely or fair
or touched with joy or desire. She's mad for sex,
but when she's got a man, she nauseates him.
A sneak, she does her neighbors enormous harm
and often eats the neglected offerings up.

Another is born from a dainty long-maned mare.
She turns up her nose at anguish and toil.
She'll neither touch the mill nor lift the sieve
nor throw the dung outside the house nor sit
beside the oven—she prefers to avoid the soot.
It's only by constraint that she takes a mate.
She washes off the dirt twice a day,
sometimes thrice, and anoints herself with myrrh.
She always wears her hair combed out long
and shadowed in its depths with flowering buds.
A lovely sight to other men is a wife
like this, but to the one that's got her
a terrible ill unless he's a tyrant or king
who can delight his soul with frivolous things.

Another from an ape. This one's the worst by far
of all the woes that Zeus has bestowed upon
humankind. She's got the ugliest face,
and as she goes through the town, she's a joke to men.

With her short neck she hunches along. She's got
no behind. She's withered of shank. Pity the man
who embraces a mischief like this. She knows all
the cunning arts and wiles, just like an ape,
nor does she care if people laugh at her.
She'll do no one any good, but this
she sees and thinks about all day long:
how she'll do the greatest possible ill.
    Another from a bee. Lucky is he
who gets one like this, for no reproach
settles on her. Life blossoms because of her
and flourishes too. Loved, she grows old
with a husband who loves her too, and bears a stock
that's lovely to see and honored of name as well.
Distinguished among womankind, a grace
that's divine suffuses her. She doesn't enjoy
sitting with women who gossip and talk about sex.
Wives like this are the wisest and best that Zeus
bestows upon mankind. Those other breeds
he made an eternal bane to humankind.
    For this is the biggest bad thing that Zeus has made:
women. For even if they seem to help,
a wife is still the greatest woe to the one
that's got her. He'll never have a cheerful day—
the one that lives with a woman—nor will he soon
thrust hunger out of doors, that housemate
of hatefulness, that hostile deity.
Whenever a man seems especially glad
at home by fate of god or grace of man,
finding fault, she'll helmet herself for war.
For where a woman is, she'll not receive
graciously a stranger who comes to the house.
She who seems especially discreet,
she's the one who's most outrageous of all.
Her husband gawks at her, but the neighbors delight
to see how still another man is deceived.
Each, when he mentions her, praises his wife
but blames the wife of another man, but still

we cannot see our equal destiny.
For this is the biggest bad thing that Zeus has made,
shackling us fast with fetters we cannot break
ever since the day that Hades embraced
those men who went to war for a woman's sake.

TYRTAIOS

10

To die is a fine thing when a noble man falls
    fighting in the forefront of battle on behalf
of his fatherland; to abandon his city and rich fields
    and go a beggar is most distressing of all,
wandering with his dear mother and ancient father,
    his little children and lawfully wedded wife.
Loathsome among those to whom he comes, enthralled
    to want and hateful poverty; a disgrace
to his line, he belies his glorious form, and all dishonor
    and every wickedness attend him.
If there be no concern for a wandering man and no
    respect or reverence or pity at all,
then let us fight, spiritedly, for our children and land,
    and let us die, no longer sparing our souls.
Standing staunch, O youths, do battle all together.
    Never think of shameful flight or fear,
but make the heart that beats in your breast mighty and stout,
    and never grow faint of heart fighting the foe.
The older men, no longer nimble of knee, do not
    abandon, taking your flight from those elder ones.
It is a shameful thing for an older man to fall
    in the foremost lines and then to lie before
the young, his head already white and his beard hoar,
    breathing forth his staunch soul to the dust,
holding his bloody genitals in his own hands—
    a sight foul to the eyes, enraging to see—
and naked his flesh, while all is seemly to lads as long
    as they have the glorious bloom of lovely youth.
A young man is a marvel for men to see, to women
    desirable as long as he lives, and fair
when he falls in forefront of battle. Let each man plant his feet
    upon the earth and bite his lip with his teeth.

HIPPONAX

115

by the billow buffeted,
at Salmydessos may the top-knotted Thracians
take him naked to eat
the bread of slavery and have his fill
of many ills, stiff
with cold, and from the foam may he tangle with
seaweed in ropes, his teeth
chattering as he lies like a dog upon
his belly, helplessly,
where the surf breaks, spewing forth the brine.
This I would like to see.
He did me wrong and trod upon his oath,
he who was once my friend.

MIMNERMOS

1

What life is there apart from golden Aphrodite?
 What joy can there be? May I die when I
no longer care for secret love and tender gifts
 and bed, the alluring blossoms of youth for men
and women too. And when miserable old age
 comes on that makes a man both ugly and mean,
then troublesome worries forever wear and tear at his wits,
 nor can he enjoy the sight of the sun's rays.
Children find him hateful, women contemptible.
 So vexatious has god made old age.

2

But we, like the leaves that bud in the blossoming season of spring
 and quickly increase beneath the beams of the sun,
like these for a cubit's length of time we take delight
 in the buds of spring, and from the gods we know
neither good nor ill. The black spirits of death stand near.
 One holds the fate of cruel old age;
the other, of death. As fleeting the season of youth's fruit
 as the sun's spreading of beams upon the earth,
but when the time for reaping the harvest is past and gone,
 then immediate death is better than life.
For many the troubles that then beset the soul. At times
 the house wastes and poverty's bitter work
is at hand. Another goes to Hades beneath the earth
 without the children for which he especially longs.
Another succumbs to soul-destroying disease. There's none
 Zeus does not give a plentitude of ills.

12

For the sun has got as his lot labor every day,
 nor is there ever any rest for him
or his horses when rosy-fingered Dawn leaves behind
 Ocean and climbs up the brightening sky,
for over the wave in a lovely spangled bed, forged
 by Hephaistos' hand of precious gold and winged,
he is borne, delightfully asleep, on the water's face
 from the country of the Hesperides
to the land of the Aithiopians, where his steeds
 and swift chariot stand until Dawn,
the early-born, appears, and the son of Hyperion
 then mounts and drives away his dazzling car.

SOLON

13

Glorious children of Memory and Olympian Zeus,
    Muses of Pieria, hear my prayer.
Grant me prosperity as a gift from the blessed gods
    and from men always a noble reputation.
May I be sweet to my friends, but bitter to my foes,
    to these a man to respect, but awful to those
to behold. Money I desire but not to acquire
    it unrighteously, for retribution
comes always afterward. The wealth gods give to a man
    is set secure from the uttermost depths to the crest,
but wealth men honor with violence indecorously
    comes, persuaded by unrighteous deeds.
It attends unwillingly and quickly is mixed
    with ruin. It begins, as it were, from a little fire,
paltry at first, but in the end a terrible thing.
    Deeds of violence endure not
for long, but Zeus oversees all, and suddenly,
    as a wind quickly scatters the clouds of spring
and stirs the depths of the billowing barren sea and wastes
    across the grain-bearing earth the lovely fields
and reaches at last the steep heavenly seat of the gods
    and makes again the sky sparkling to see,
and the strength of the sun lights the lovely rich land,
    nor are there any clouds left to see—
like this is the vengeance of Zeus. Not like a mortal man
    for every single thing is he quick to wrath,
but forever aware is he of the man who has a soul
    that sins, and he makes him obvious in the end.
One pays straightway, another at a later day.
    God's fate may not overtake the men themselves
who escape but comes in time nevertheless, and, guiltless,
    their children pay for their sins or afterward

their progeny. For thus we mortals think, good
    and bad alike, each his own favoring thought,
until he suffers. Then he grieves. Before this,
    gaping, we delight in frivolous hopes.
And so the man oppressed by cruel disease expects
    that he'll be well. This is what he thinks.
Another cowardly soul thinks that he is brave,
    and handsome thinks himself the homely man.
The one who lacks means, constrained by poverty,
    expects nevertheless to acquire wealth
in plenty. Each has his own pursuit. One on the sea
    wanders in ships, longing to bring home
gain. Borne on the fishy depths by cruel winds,
    he does not spare his soul, not in the least.
Another cleaves the thickly wooded land for a year,
    serving those whose concern is the curved plow.
Another gleans his livelihood skilled with his hands
    in the works of Athena and Hephaistos of many crafts;
another taught in the gifts of the Olympian Muses,
    knowing the measure of lovely wisdom of song.
Another the lord Apollo, the archer from afar,
    has made a seer who knows the evil to come,
for the gods accompany him, but what is destined to be
    neither augury nor sacrifice
will fend off. Others, physicians, have the task
    of Paion of many medicines. For them
there is no end, for often from a trifling pain
    there comes enormous agony, nor can
one ease it with soothing drugs, although with touch of hands
    one can restore the suffering man to health
immediately. To mortal men Fate brings both good
    and ill, and inescapable are the gifts
of the deathless gods. There's danger in every deed, nor does
    one know from its beginning a matter's end,
but the man who tries to do good, unforeseeing, falls
    into enormous and harsh disaster, but to the man
who does evil god gives everything good
    and fortunate, an escape from his foolishness.

No limit of wealth is prescribed for men, for those of us
who have the greatest livelihood are twice
as greedy as other men. Who could satiate all?
Surely the deathless gods grant us gain,
but when Zeus in retribution for that sends
disaster, one man's loss is another's gain.

THEOGNIS

39–52

Kyrnos, this city's with child. I fear that she'll bring forth
  a chastiser of our evil violence,
for though the citizens are sensible, their leaders
  are on their way to enormous wickedness.
Kyrnos, never yet have its nobles destroyed a city,
  but whenever violence pleases the base, and they
corrupt the commons and give judgment to unjust men
  for the sake of power and private gain, do not
expect that city to be untroubled for long, not even
  if now she lies in utter tranquility,
whenever these to evil men become dear—
  gains that come to the common folk for ill.
From such come revolutions and internecine gore
  and tyrannies. Our city may these never please.

183–92

Kyrnos, we look for thoroughbred asses and steeds
  and wish from the best to breed our good stock.
But a noble man doesn't scruple to marry a base wife
  from a base sire if he gives money in plenty,
nor does a woman refuse to be the wedded wife
  of a base man if he is rich. She prefers
wealth to good. It's money they honor. A noble man
  marries from base stock; the bad from the good.
Wealth corrupts the breed. Don't wonder that the citizens' line
  grows dim, for noble things are mixed with the base.

667–82

If I had the money, Simonides, I used to have,
  I would not be grieved in company with the good,

but now it passes me by, who knew it once, and I
    am speechless for want, though I know better than most
that now we are borne, swept with our snowy sails down,
    from out the Melian sea through the murk of night,
nor will they bail out. The sea washes over both
    the ship's sides. Their actions will scarcely save
a single soul. They hinder the noble steersman
    who understands the keeping of watch and seize
by force the cargo of wealth. Order perishes,
    and there's no longer equal division of goods.
The porters are in command; the nobles subjected to base.
    I fear that a wave will swallow down our ship.
This is the cryptic riddle I give to noble men,
    but the base will get it too if they have wit.

949–54

I did not drink the blood of the fawn that I tore with my claws
    like a lion sure of its strength from its mother the hind.
I climbed the towering walls but did not sack the town.
    I yoked the steeds but did not mount the car.
Acting, I did not act. Completing, I did not complete.
    Achieving, I did not achieve. Doing, I didn't.

ALKMAN

I

There is a vengeance of gods.
Blessed is he who blithely
weaves his day straight through
without a tear. But I sing
the light of Agido. I see
her like the sun that Agido
summons up to shine
on us. Our glorious leader
allows me neither to praise
nor blame her at all. She knows
that she herself stands forth,
as though one set among the herds
a well-built steed, a bringer
of prizes with pounding hooves,
a creature of dreams with wings.

Do you see her? That courser
is Venetic. But the hair
of my cousin Hagesichora
blossoms like gold unalloyed.
As for her silvery face—
must I make it so plain?
This is Hagesichora.
But she who is second in beauty
to Agido runs like a Kolaxaian
courser beside an Ibenian
steed. The Peleiades,
as we carry her plow to Orthria
through the ambrosial night,
like Sirius the star,
rise up and fight with us.

There is no abundance
of purple that can protect us,

nor snake though spangled all
in gold, nor Lydian cap
that flatters soft-eyed girls,
nor can Nanno's locks,
nor Areta, a goddess to see,
nor Sylakis, nor Kleësithera,
nor can you go to Ainesimbrota's
and say, "Give me Astaphis,
and let Philylla look at me,
and Demareta, and lovely Ianthemis."
It is Hagesichora for whom we pine.

For is the lovely-ankled
Hagesichora not here?
Does she not stand next to Agido
and praise with her our festival?
To gods belong the fulfillment
and end. O choir leader,
I tell you that I, a girl,
have shrieked in vain from the beams,
like an owl, though I long to please Dawn
most of all. For she it is
who heals our pains.
From Hagesichora the girls
have come upon the peace
for which they longed.

For so the others have run
beside their trace horse.
The captain must have on board
his ship a strong voice.
She does not sing the Sirens
down, for they are gods.
Instead of eleven children
we are ten. She sings upon
the streams of Xanthos like a swan.
But she with the lovely yellow hair . . .

3

The lovely song . . .
of the singers . . .
will scatter sweet sleep
from my eyes . . .
and leads me to the contest
where I shall shake my yellow hair . . .

. . . .

with longing that looses the limbs
she gives glances more melting
than sleep or death . . .

. . . .

and not vainly is she sweet . . .
. . . Astymeloisa gives me no answer,
but bringing a wreath,
like a star that falls
down the glittering sky,
or a golden shoot,
or a delicate feather,
she has come . . .
with long steps . . .

. . . .

The dewy grace of Kinyras
is set upon the maidens' hair.

14c

falls upon the shore,
dumb among the bracken.

16

He was not a rustic man,
nor a clumsy one,
nor Thessalian by birth,
nor a shepherd from Erysiche,
but from steep Sardis . . .

17

In time I'll give you a cauldron.
It's unfired still, but soon
it will fill with thick pea soup,
the kind that that glutton Alkman
loves lukewarm when the solstice
has come. He doesn't eat
the fancy stuff but seeks
the common fare, what the people
have . . .

19

Seven couches and
as many tables, crowned
with cakes of poppy seed,
of linseed and sesame too,
and there among the cups
confections of honey and flax

20

Seasons he made three,
summer, winter, fall.
The fourth was spring,
when things thrive but
one can't eat his fill.

26

No longer, girls of honey-tongued words, of holy voice,
can my limbs support me. Oh, would that I were the halcyon
who flies over the crest of the wave with the kingfishers,
keeping a fearless heart, the sea-purple sacred bird.

27

Come, Muse, Kalliope,
daughter of Zeus,
begin your lovely lines
and make a song
to please us and a dance
that will charm.

29

And I shall sing,
starting from Zeus.

30

The Muse sang out,
the shrill Siren . . .

38

As many of us
as are young
praise our
lyre player.

39

Alkman found lyric
and song by noting
the tongued trill
of partridges.

40

I know the songs
of all the birds.

41

There inches against the iron
the lyre beautifully played.

42

eating nectar

47

Did I see Phoibos
then in a dream?

50b

Ino, queen of the sea,
from her breasts . . .

53

Clad in the skins
of wild beasts

55

Leaving lovely Kypros
and Paphos where the sea washes . . .

56

Many times on the tops of mountains, when
gods were glad at their torchlit feasts,
you took a golden pail, a great can,
like one that shepherds have,
and putting lion's milk inside,
you made a cheese, a big one, unbroken,
for Argeïphontes . . .

57

Such are the things
that the daughter of Zeus
and the shining Moon,
Dew, makes grow.

58

It is not Aphrodite, but lustful love
that plays like a child, treading upon
the blossom tops—touch them not,
I beg of you—of galingale.

59a

At Aphrodite's command Love
distills and melts my heart.

59b

Blond Megalostrata,
blessed among girls,
has shown this gift
of the sweet Muses.

60

And I pray to you,
bearing this garland
of helichryse and
lovely galingale.

64

Of Persuasion and Order the sister,
of Forethought the daughter.

68

With polished spear Ajax raves
and Memnon lusts for blood.

77

Paris the wicked,
Paris the grim,
Evil to Hellas,
nurse of men.

79

That sinner sat among delights
upon a seat beneath a rock and saw
nothing at all, but thought that he did.

80

Kirke once, when she had anointed the ears
of the comrades of Odysseus, stout of heart . . .

81

I wish, father Zeus, that he were my husband.

82

The girls sank down,
helplessly,
like birds beneath
a hovering hawk.

89

The mountain peaks are asleep and the chasms.
The torrents sleep and the forelands.

Asleep is all the creeping breed that dark earth feeds,
the mountain beasts and the race of bees.
Monsters sleep in the depths of the purple sea.
Asleep too is the tribe
of the long-winged birds.

90

Rhipe, mountain
budding with woods,
breast of black night.

91

She wears a necklace of gold
with petals of delicate purple.

93

The parti-colored bird
destroys the vine buds.

94

lettuce loaves and loaves like breasts

95a

mourned at the mill
and common meal

95b

And Alkman made himself a meal.

96

Soon he will offer
pulse and porridge
and white whey
and the waxy fruit
of the bees.

100

smaller than a quince

102

The path is narrow
and necessity pitiless.

104

Who with ease could read
the mind of another man?

108

a brackish neighborhood

110

You are like ripe flax.

117

She wears a lovely linen gown.

125

Trial, you know,
is the start
of Wisdom.

127

earring

STESICHOROS

178

Hermes gave them Flame
and Snatcher, fleet
offspring of Whitefoot,
and Hera Blondie
and Bowlegs.

179a

sesame cakes and gruel,
cakes of honey and oil,
pastries of other kinds,
and honey of pale gold

179b

In the jumping,
Amphiaraos,
but with the javelin,
Meleager
carried off the prize.

180

hand-gnawing bond

181

Taking the cupped bowl, three flagons deep,
he put it to his lips and drank what Pholos
the centaur had mixed and set beside him.

184

near famed Erytheia
beside the silver-rooted, boundless springs
of the river Tartessos, in a hollow of rock

185

Helios, the son of Hyperion, embarked
in his golden cup, that he might cross the Ocean
and come to the depths of dark and holy night,
to his mother, his wedded wife, and his dear sons.
But Herakles entered the grove, shadowed with laurel,
on foot, the son of Zeus.

186

six hands and six feet and wings

187

Many Kydonian quinces they tossed
at the chariot of the king,
and many myrtle boughs
and garlands of roses
and twisted wreaths of violets.

188

a footbath of silvery stone

192

That story is not true.
You did not sail in the well-benched ships.
You did not go to the fortress of Troy.

200

for the daughter of Zeus pitied him
forever bearing water to the kings.

210

Muse, thrust aside wars and sing with me
the marriages of gods, the feasts of men,
and the celebrations of the blest.

211

when in the spring the swallow babbles

212

We must find a Phrygian tune
to sing songs like these
of the lovely-haired Graces,
delicately, when spring comes on.

219

There appeared to her a serpent with bloodied crest,
and from it was born a king of the Pleisthenid line.

221

hid the tip
of his snout beneath the earth

223

Once Tyndareus
sacrificed to all the gods, but forgot
Aphrodite alone, the lady of gracious gifts.

Angered with the daughters of Tyndareus,
she made them twice married, thrice married,
and forsakers of husbands.

232

Apollo loves the musicians'
merrymakings and song.
Hades got as his lot
lamentings and grief.

235

Poseidon, prince of the hollow-hooved horses

240

Come here,
Kalliope,
of the high
sweet voice.

242

you yourself first,
fighter at the gate

243

sent the slender javelins

244

hopeless and useless to weep for the dead

245

When a man dies,
all his grace
among men
also dies.

255

an unbounded barking of dogs

278

Come, tuneful Muse,
begin the lovely song
of the children of Samos,
sounding aloud
on your lovely lyre.

S 15

. . . held a shield
from his head . . .
. . . horsehaired helmet
. . . to the ground
. . . of hateful . . .
death . . .
having about his head, polluted
with gore . . . in anger
the pangs of man-destroying Hydra
of spangled neck. In silence,
with stealth, he stove in its brow
and split the flesh and bones
by divinity's decree.
His arrow pierced straight through
the very peak of its head
and stained with red-brown blood
its breast and gory limbs.

He bent back the neck of Geryon,
aslant, as when a poppy,
disgracing its delicate form,
casts its petals away . . .

IBYKOS

282

Dardanian Priam's city, famed,
enormous and blessed, they destroyed, sped
from Argos, by counsel of mighty Zeus,

for beauty of Helen of tawny hair
with strife much to be sung in a war
bewept, and disaster mounted the walls
of suffering Pergamon because
of Kypris, the goddess of golden hair.

Now neither host-deceiving Paris
nor slender-ankled Kassandra is it
my desire to sing . . .
or the other children of Priam the king

or the taking of Troy of the high gates
on a nameless day, for never yet . . .
heroes' excessive bravery
    whom hollow

ships, bolted well, brought,
noble heroes, a bane to Troy.
Lord Agamemnon, leader of men,
a Pleisthenid and king, a son
of noble Atreus, commanded them.

Upon such the Muses, skilled in song,
the daughters of Helikon, might well
embark. No mortal man alive
could tell every single deed

of ships, how Menelaos came
together with his men from Aulis
across the Aegean Sea from Argos
to horse-rearing [Troy] . . .

brazen-shielded Achaians' sons
of whom foremost of those with the spear

was Achilles, swift of foot . . .
and Telamonian Ajax, mighty and stout

. . . from Argos
. . . to Ilion

. . . golden-girt
Hyllis was, to whom Trojans
and Danaans compared Troilos
in his lovely form as one would

gold thrice refined to bronze.
Beauty will be forever theirs,
and you, Polykrates, will have
undying fame, and I as well
shall have renown because of my song.

283

sat beside him
for a long time,
frozen in wonder

285

The boys with white steeds,
children of Molione, I killed,
of like age, one size, single
of limb, born both of them
in a silver egg.

286

In spring Kydonian quinces
are watered by river streams,
there where the Maids
keep their garden unshorn
and the vine blossom swells
beneath the leaves'
shadowing spray.

But for me
there is no season
the Love God sleeps.
For from beneath
the lightning's blaze,
like the North Wind from Thrace,
he leaps from the Kyprian's side.
Black, bold,
with shriveling madness,
he shakes
and utterly shatters
my soul.

287

Again Love from beneath his blue-black brows
    gives me a melting glance
and with manifold spells catches me
    in Aphrodite's unending net.
Truly I tremble at his approach like an old
yoke-bearing, prizewinning horse who goes,
all unwilling, now with the swift car to the fray.

288

Euryalos, sprig of the gleaming Graces,
darling of those of the lovely hair,
Kypris and soft-eyed Persuasion
reared you among blossoms of rose.

302

He lay beside a Kadmeian girl.

303a

The talk of men
constrains Kassandra,

Priam's gray-eyed
daughter who has
the lovely hair.

303b

When glorious Dawn
that puts an end to sleep
wakes the nightingales

310

I fear that sinning somehow
in the eyes of the gods
I'll buy honor from men.

311a

having a mouth lustful for Strife

311b

he may helmet battle against me

312

being about to drink
fast-falling drops of rain

313

You cannot find for the dead
a drug to restore them to life.

314

blazing through the long night
like the gleaming stars

315

violets and myrtle and helichryse,
apples and roses and the glossy bay

316

loosing their embroidered robes
and their brooches and veils

317a

In its topmost leaves
sit the pied wild ducks
and the gleaming-necked
shag-purples and the long-
winged halcyons.

317b

always to me,
O my soul,
like the wide-winged
purple bird

321

to the dry land
built by mortal hands
where once there dwelt
with the sea snails
flesh-gnawing fish

330

Beyond the crest of the wave
every reefing rope is safe.

337

an army clad in skins

338

dogs about the table

SAPPHO

I

Deathless Aphrodite of dazzling throne,
beguiling enchantress, child of Zeus, do not,
I beseech you, overwhelm my soul with torment
and anguish, O queen,

but come here to me, if ever before
you heard from afar my voice and listened to me,
and, abandoning your father's golden home,
you came to me,

your chariot yoked, and your sparrows, pretty and swift,
with frequent pulsing of fluttering wings bore you
athwart the black earth, sheer from above,
through heaven's mist,

and quickly they came, and you, O blessed one,
with a smile upon your immortal face, asked
whatever I suffered now and why again
I called on you

and whatever I most in my maddened heart wanted
to happen to me. "Whom am I now to persuade
to lead you back to her love? Who, O Sappho,
does you wrong?

"For if she flees, she'll soon pursue, and if
she refuses gifts, she'll soon bestow them.
And if she does not love, soon she will,
in her despite."

Come to me even now and release me
from torturing cares, and all that my heart
desires, accomplish for me, and do you yourself
do battle with me.

2

Come to me from Crete, down from heaven,
come, for here your shrine in a charming
grove of apple trees keeps its altars
smoking with incense.

Here the water, cool through the apple
boughs, is babbling; shadowed with roses
all the grove. From shimmering leaves sleep,
drifting, will come down.

Here a meadow pasturing horses
blooms with flowers promising springtime.
Breezes blow with breath that is sweet, like
honey from good bees.

Taking here the garlands, O Kypris,
pour in golden cups, do it gently,
nectar mixed with our celebration,
pour it like fine wine.

5

Grant, O
Kypris, and Nereids too, that all
unharmed my brother come back, that all in his heart
he wishes to happen to him come at last
to fulfillment,

that he atone for all the harm he did
before and be a delight to his friends but doom
to enemies, and may no one be again
a grief to us,

and may he wish to make his sister endowed
with honor . . .

15

Kypris, may she find you bitter too
and not boast, saying this:

"How desirable a love has Doricha found,
coming again this second time."

16

A host of horsemen, some say, is the loveliest sight
upon the black earth; some say a display
of soldiery; some, a fleet of ships, but I say
it's whomever one loves.

It is very simple to make this understood
to all, for she who surpassed in loveliness
all mortal men, Helen, abandoned her spouse,
a very noble man,

and went sailing off to Troy and gave
no thought at all to her child or beloved parents,
but Aphrodite led her lightly astray . . .

. . . .

She reminds me now of Anaktoria . . .
who is no longer here,

and I would rather see her lovely walk
and the sparkle of her shining countenance
than Lydian chariots battling in armament.

22

I bid you, take your lyre,
Abanthis, and sing of Gongyla,
while longing for her, the lovely one,
flutters your heart . . .

for the sight of her dress excited you,
and I rejoice, for the sacred Kypros-
born reproached me once because
I made this prayer to her . . .

23

For when I see you opposite me,
not even Hermione seems to compare,
and to liken you to tawny-
haired Helen is not unseemly at all.

27

for you were once a child . . .
come and sing of this and talk
and grant us lovely favors . . .

We're going to a wedding—
you know this well—so
send away the virgins
as quickly as you can,
and may the gods have . . .
To mighty Olympos
for mortals . . .
there is no road.

29

Gorgo's necklaces and robes

30

All night long the girls
may sing of your love
for the bride of violet gown.

But now wake up! Go bring
the lusty bachelors
who are as young as you
that we may get less sleep
than the trilling nightingale.

31

That man seems to me to be a god
who sits opposite you and listens to
you speaking so sweetly and close to him
and hears you too

laughing delightfully. Truly that flutters
the heart in my breast, for when for a moment I look
at you, I cannot speak at all; my tongue
is benumbed,

and a subtle flame runs immediately
beneath my flesh. My eyes see nothing at all
before them and in my ears there is a noise
of humming tops.

Sweat pours down and drenches me, and I
am all atremble and turner greener than grass
is, and I am, as far as I can see,
almost dead.

32

who brought me honor
with the gift of their works

33

O Aphrodite of the golden wreath,
I wish that such luck were mine!

34

Stars around the lovely moon
hide their gleaming beauty away
whenever she at the full sheds
over the earth her radiant glow.

35

Either Panormos or Kypros or Paphos

39

An embroidered shoe,
a lovely Lydian work,
covered her foot.

40

I sacrifice to you
. . . of a white goat.

41

Toward you beautiful girls
my thought is unalterable.

42

The heart of the doves grows chill,
and they slacken their wings.

44

A herald came, Idaios, the swift messenger

. . . .

of all Asia . . . imperishable renown . . .
"Hektor and his companions are bringing from holy Thebe
and Plakia the dainty, dark-eyed Andromache
in ships upon the salt sea together with
many bracelets of gold and crimson robes
and trinkets wrought with very intricate design
and countless silver drinking cups and ivory too."
So he spoke, and nimbly his dear father leapt up,

and the story went throughout the wide citadel
to his friends, and straightway the sons of Ilos harnessed
mules to wagons with good wheels, and all the crowd
of women and slender-ankled girls climbed up,
and in another place the daughters of Priam yoked
horses to chariots . . .

and heroes and godlike charioteers, and all in a crowd
they set out for holy Ilion . . .

Sweet melodies of flute mingled with the clash
of castanets, and the maidens sang a sacred song,
and there came to the sky a heavenly echo, and everywhere
along the road were mixing bowls and drinking cups,
and frankincense and cassia and myrrh mingled together,
and the women, those who were older, raised a cry, and all
the men gave the lovely shrill shout and called
on Paion, the Far-archer, who has the lovely lyre,
and sang of Hektor and Andromache, who were
in their happiness exactly like the heavenly gods.

46

Upon luxurious cushions
I'll lay my limbs down.

47

Love shook
my heart like the wind
that down the mountain
batters the oak.

48

You came, and I was mad for you,
but you chilled my heart aflame with desire.

49

I loved you once, Atthis,
a long time ago.
You seemed to me then
a small child
without any grace.

50

He who is fair is fair
as far as seeing goes,
but he who is good will
in time be also fair.

51

I know not what to do.
I'm of two minds.

52

I couldn't hope
to touch the sky
with my two hands.

53

Rosy-armed Graces,
pure daughters of Zeus,
come here to us.

54

Love came from heaven
clad in crimson cloak.

55

You will die and no one will remember you,
for you've had no share in the roses of Pieria,
but you will drift here and there, unseen,
in Hades' house, and flutter about
among the dark, not illustrious dead.

56

I do not think that any girl
who looks upon the sun's light
will be skilled as you in her art.

57

What country girl
in country clothes
inflames your heart,
though she doesn't know
how to make her dress
come down to her feet?

58

Age withers now my flesh,
and my black locks are white.
No longer do my knees
carry me to dance
like a tender young fawn.

But I love delicacy,
and brightness and beauty
belong for me
to a passion for sunlight.

81

And you, Dika, bind lovely garlands
about your locks, twining sprigs of anise
with your tender hands, for the blessed Graces prefer
to see beautifully blossoming things and turn
aside from those who go ungarlanded.

82

Mnasidika, lovelier
in form than Gyrinno
of the tender flesh

91

Irana, I've never come upon
anyone more disdainful than you.

94

Truly I wish I were dead.
She wept much when she left me
and said, "This is cruel, Sappho.
Against my will I leave you."
But I answered her this,
"Go with good cheer. Remember me.
You know how I've cherished you.
If not, I want to remind you
of the happiness we've had.
Often, when you were with me,
you put on your hair
wreaths of roses and violets,
and around your delicate neck
plaited garlands of buds.
You anointed your skin
with precious myrrh
and royal balm.

On a soft couch
you quenched your desire
for tender . . ."

95

Gongyla

I said, "O lord,
by the blessed goddess,
I have no pleasure
in being above the earth.
A longing takes me
to die and see
the dewy banks
of Acheron
where the lotus grows."

96

Sardis, . . .
where often she turns her thought . . .

She'd compare you to a goddess
and take delight in your dancing,
but . . .
Now she shines among
Lydian women, as when,
after the sun has set,
the rosy-fingered moon
is more radiant than all
the stars. She pours her light
upon the salt sea
and on the flowering fields.
The lovely dew is spread,
and roses come to bloom
and delicate anthriscus
and budding melilot.
Often she wanders to

and fro, remembering
gentle Atthis. Desire
gnaws at her tender heart.

98

My mother used to say,
when I was just your age,
that a girl who bound her hair
with a purple band wore
the most becoming thing
that any girl could wear.

But for the girl whose hair
is more yellow than torches
wreaths of flowering buds
are more becoming by far.

Not long ago I had
a broad embroidered band
from Sardis. But for you,
Kleïs, I have no colored
band, nor do I know
where I shall get one.

100

and wrapped her well
with delicate linen

101

crimson scented scarves
she sent from Phokaia,
expensive gifts

102

Mother, I cannot strike my loom. I'm undone
by my love for a boy by delicate Aphrodite.

104

Evening, you bring back all that the Dawn scatters abroad.
You bring back the sheep,
you bring back the goat, you bring to its mother
the child.

105

Like the sweet apple that reddens on the topmost bough,
at the top of the topmost—the apple pickers forgot it.
No, they did not forget it. They could not get it.

Like the mountain hyacinth that shepherds trample
underfoot, and on the ground the purple blossom . . .

106

Superior, as the Lesbian bard to foreigners

107

Do I long still for my maidenhood?

110

Seven fathoms long
the doorkeeper's feet;
of five oxhides
his shoes, and ten
were the cobblers
that struggled
to cobble them.

111

Lift high the roof beam—
Hymenaios!
Lift it high, O carpenter men—
Hymenaios!
The bridegroom comes.
Like Ares is he—
bigger far than a man.

112

Bridegroom, you are blessed.
Your marriage accomplished,
just as you prayed, the girl too
for whom you prayed . . .
"You are charming to see; your eyes . . .
gentle, and love suffuses
your beautiful face." Aphrodite
honors you exceedingly.

113

For there never was another girl,
O bridegroom, like this one.

114

Maidenhood, maidenhood,
where have you gone,
abandoning me?
Never again shall I come
to you. Never again.

115

To what, dear bridegroom, shall I compare you?
To a tender sapling I can best compare you.

117

Good-bye to the bride! Good-bye to the groom!

118

But come,
my heavenly lute,
take voice.

120

For I am not spiteful
but have the heart
of an innocent child.

121

If you care for me, then win
the bed of a younger woman,
for I will not endure to be
the elder in a love affair.

122

A delicate girl
plucking buds.

123

In golden sandals Dawn
had just come to me.

124

you yourself, Kalliope

125

I myself wove garlands once.

126

May you sleep
upon the breast
of a tender friend.

128

Now come, O delicate Graces
and Muses of lovely hair.

129

Have you forgotten me,
or do you love some other
more than you do me?

130

Love that looses my limbs shakes me again,
the bittersweet, irresistible, creeping thing.

131

Atthis, you've come to hate the thought of me.
You go fluttering after Andromeda now.

132

I have a lovely daughter.
She looks like a blossom of gold.
Her name is Kleïs. For her
I'd not take all of Lydia
nor even enchanting . . .

133

Andromeda makes a fair exchange.

134

I spoke with you
in a dream,
O Kypros-born.

135

Why, O Irana,
does the daughter
of Pandion,
the swallow . . .

136

Messenger of spring,
his voice desire,
the nightingale

137

There's something I want to say
to you but shame forbids.

"But if you longed for what
was honorable or good,
and if your tongue were not
whipping up evil to say,
you'd not cover your eyes
in shame; you'd state your claim."

138

If you care for me,
stand opposite me
and spread the charm
that is in your eyes.

140

Delicate Adonis dies,
Kythereia.
What are we to do?
Beat your breasts,
O maids,
and rend your robes.

141

There a bowl of ambrosia
had been mixed, and Hermes
took the pitcher and poured
it like wine for the gods.
They all had drinking cups
and poured libations and prayed
for everything good for the groom.

142

Leto and Niobe were best of friends.

143

Golden pulse bloomed upon the shore.

144

with more
than their fill
of Gorgo

145

Don't move the pebble piles.

146

For me neither honey nor bee

147

Someone, I say,
afterward,
will remember us.

148

Wealth without excellence
is not a harmless neighbor.
A mixture of both brings
the best of blessedness.

150

There ought not to be
threnodies in
the house of the Muses'
attendants, for such
would surely not
be fitting for us.

151

The black sleep of the night
cloaks my eyes.

152

mingled with colors of every kind

154

The full moon appeared
and the girls took their stand
all around the altar.

155

I wish the child
of Polyanax' house
many a joy.

156

more sweetly tuned
than the lyre
by far

and more golden
than gold

158

Beware the vainly barking tongue
when rage spreads in the chest.

159

You and my servant Love

160

And now I shall sing
these songs, beautifully,
to delight my friends.

161

Guard her, bridegrooms,
kings of citadels.

166

They say that Leda once
found hidden
an egg of hyacinthine
blue.

167

whiter far than an egg

168

for Adonis, woe

168b

The moon has gone
and the Seven Stars.
The midnight hours
go by, while I,
I lie alone.

168c(?)

brindled the earth
of many wreaths

192

goblets, gold-bossed

ALKAIOS

6

This billow now comes like the one before
and we will be terribly hard put
to bail it out when it washes overboard,

so let us strengthen our hull as quickly as
we can and race for a harbor that's safe and secure,

and let not cowardly reluctance seize
upon any one of us, for it's obvious
that an enormous challenge faces us.
Remember our earlier suffering and let

every man stand steadfast and let
us not disgrace with lack of manliness
our noble parents who lie beneath the earth.

10b

I am a wretched woman
and have my share of all
the evils of the house
and its disgraceful destiny.

I am incurably maimed.

The belling of the stag
springs in the timid heart
of the hind . . . maddened
. . . infatuate . . .

34

Come here to me, abandoning Pelops' isle,
mighty sons of Zeus and Leda. Appear

with favoring heart, O Kastor, propitiously,
and Polydeukes,

who gallop over the broad earth and all
the salt sea upon your fleet-footed steeds
and rescue easily from chilling death
mortal men,

leaping upon the prows of their well-benched ships,
luminous afar as you run up
the rigging and bring light in the cruel night
to the black ship.

38a

Drink and be drunk, Melanippos, with me. Why
do you suppose that once you've crossed the swirling ford

of Acheron you'll see again the sun's
brilliant light? Don't aspire to the great,

for Aiolid Sisyphos, wisest of men,
supposed that he could master death,

but clever though he was, twice he crossed
at death's command swirling Acheron,

and Zeus contrived a labor for him
beneath the black earth. Expect not such.

For now, if ever, while we are young, we must
endure the suffering god grants to us.

42

This is how the story goes.
Once because of wicked deeds
there came to Priam and his sons
bitter grief

from you, Helen, and Zeus destroyed
sacred Ilion with fire.
Not such was the dainty girl Aiakos'
noble son

brought from the halls of Nereus and took
to Chiron's house when he called all
the blessed ones to his wedding feast.
He loosed the robe

of the pure girl. The love of Peleus
and the best of the daughters of Nereus bloomed
and within a year she bore the best
of demigods

to Peleus, a son, the blessed driver
of bay colts, but those, the Phrygians,
because of Helen, perished with
their citadel.

44

Achilles called his mother by name,
a naiad and noblest of sea nymphs.
She grasped the knees of Zeus and begged
that he acknowledge and benefit
the wrath of her beloved son.

45

Hebros, loveliest of rivers, beside Ainos
you pour into the purple sea
a shining flood of Thracian foam,
and many girls stand beside you
and with delicate hands make smooth
the flesh of their lovely thighs,
pouring your water upon them
as though it were some soothing cure.

50

Drench my head that's suffered long
with myrrh and also my hoar chest,
and let them drink . . .

69

The Lydians, father Zeus, indignant at
the way things went, presented us with two
thousand staters, hoping that we could storm
the holy city,
even though they'd not got anything good
from us nor knew us. But he, like a crafty fox,
supposed that we'd forget that he'd foretold
easy success.

70

The merrymaking lyre
attends the banquet and feasts
with idle charlatans.

Let that one who married
an Atreid devour
the city as he did
with Myrsilos, until
it pleases Ares to turn . . .

Let us slacken from
soul-gnawing strife
and internecine war,
which some Olympian
has roused among us,
ruining the folk
but bringing to Pittakos
the glory that he craves.

71

You were my friend.
I invited you
for kid and pork.
Such is the custom.

72

violently . . .
they fill it with unmixed wine,
and night and day it seethes,
where frequently the custom . . .

That man did not forget
all this when first he turned
things upside down and kept
night after night awake
with the ladle ringing against
the bottom of the jug.

Do you, born of such
a mother, suppose that you
have the honor of men
who were born free and from
aristocratic stock?

73

all the cargo . . .
as much as possible . . .

She has no desire, she says, to be
smitten by a billow and do
battle with the rain and be
shattered upon an unseen reef.

Let her then be on her way.
I want to forget all this, my friends,
to be young and joyous with all of you
and with Bykchis . . .

and so, until tomorrow, we . . .

119

For now your time has passed you by,
and the fruit, what there was of it, is plucked,
but perhaps the shoot, for it is fine,

will bear abundant clusters of grapes,
but I fear the harvesters will pluck
from such a vine unripe grapes.

129

The Lesbians made this sanctuary,
spacious and conspicuous,
and built within it altars of
the blessed and deathless divinities

and gave their names to Zeus, God
of Suppliants, and Hera to you,
Aiolian, Glorious, Mother of All,
and Kemelios, Eater of Raw Flesh,

they called Dionysos. Come, hear,
propitiously, our prayers and save
us from burdens and cruel banishment

and let their Fury pursue the son
of Hyrrhas, since once we swore and slit
a victim's throat never to
abandon a single of our companions

but either to die, cloaked in earth,
at the hands of those who attacked us
or afterward, murdering them, to save
the people from their wretched distress.

But Potbelly Pittakos did not
speak to their souls but casually
tramples oaths underfoot and now
he devours our city . . .

130b

Miserable that I am.
I live a country bumpkin's life
and long to hear the assembly called,
O Agesilaidas,

and the senate, and from the property
my father and my father's father have
still in old age, though among
destructive men, I'm driven away,

an exile, beyond the pale, and live
like Onomakles alone here
in the wolf thickets . . . war . . .
to rid of strife . . .

. . . to the precinct of the blessed gods,
treading upon the black earth . . .
meetings themselves, I dwell and keep
my feet outside calamity

where Lesbian women go, trailing
their robes and judged for loveliness,
and around there rings the heavenly sound
of the women's sacred annual shout.

140

The huge house blazes with bronze.
All the roof is decked for Ares
with flashing helmets that nod with white
horsehair plumes, adornments for heroes'
heads, and gleaming bronze greaves
conceal their pegs, defenses against
powerful shafts, and corselets
of new linen and hollow shields
are stacked and Chalkidian swords,
and beside them many belts and kilts.
These we can't forget since first
we undertook this dangerous task.

208

both my feet entangled in
the rigging. This is my only hope.

249

It is better not to check
the force of the winds' blast.

From land one ought to foresee
the voyage, if one can
and has the skill, but on
the deep, to run with the wind.

283

fluttered Argive Helen's heart
in her breast. Mad for the Trojan man,
who betrayed his host, she sailed with him
over the main

and left her child bereft in her house
and her husband's bed, beautifully strewn,
for Aphrodite persuaded her heart
to yield to Love.

. . . his many brothers
the black earth covers, slain
upon the Trojan plain, and all
because of her.

Many chariots crashed in the dust,
and many glancing-eyed Achaians
were trampled. Achilles glutted on gore.

296a

Did he not, like a lion,
deserve to be flayed?

296b

Kypros-born, Damoanektides . . .

beside the lovely olive trees
there drifted down delights, for when

the gates of spring are opened, boys
scented with ambrosia, and youths
garlanded in hyacinths . . .

298

shaming those who did wrong,
we must cast a noose about their necks
and after that stone them to death.

Truly it would have been better by far
had the Achaians killed that man
who defied the gods, and so sailed
past Aigai upon a calmer sea.

But in the temple Priam's daughter
embraced the image of Athena
of Much Booty and touched its chin
while the enemy sacked the citadel.

. . . Deïphobus too
they slew, and wailing arose from the walls,
and the children's shrilling cries filled
all the dusty Dardanian plain.

Ajax in lethal insanity came
to the shrine of sacred Pallas, who
of all the blessed immortals is
most awful to sacrilegious men.

With both his hands he seized the girl
as she stood beside the sacred image
and raped her, Lokrian Ajax, nor did
he fear the daughter of Zeus, the gorgon-

eyed, bestower of honors in war.
But she, scowling terribly, swept,
livid, across the wine-sparkling sea
and stirred up sudden and hidden squalls.

304

golden-haired Phoibos, whom the daughter
of Koios bore when she had lain
with the son of Kronos of mighty name,
Zeus who dwells in the clouds on high.
But Artemis swore the gods' great oath:
"By your beard, I shall always be chaste,
never wed, a huntress upon the peaks
of those mountains where no one goes.
Come, nod, give your grace to my prayer."
She spoke, and the father of the blessed ones
nodded assent. Now men and gods
call the maiden the Huntress of Deer,
Lady of the Wild, a glorious name,
and Love never comes near her.

308b

Hail, O you who rule Kyllene, for you
I wish to sing, whom Maia bore upon
the very mountain peaks when she had lain
with Zeus, Kronos' son, the king of all.

318

He put on Skythian shoes.

319

stormless breezes of weak winds

322

From Teian cups the wine drops fly.

325

Queen Athena, staunch in battle
who rule Koronea . . .
before the temple . . .
beside the banks
of the river Koralios

326

I cannot understand the list
of the wind. A billow rolls from here,
another from there, and we between
are borne away with our black ship,

belabored much by the mighty storm.
The bilge covers the mast-hold.
The sail is all transparent now.
There are enormous rips in it,

the anchors are working loose, the rudders . . .

327

most terrible of gods,
whom beautifully sandaled Iris bore
when she had lain with Zephyros
of the golden hair

329

He had a helmet
spangled with gold
and nimble . . .

332

Now we must get drunk
and drink with all our might,
since Myrsilos is dead.

333

Wine is a look-see into man.

334

Poseidon had not yet
smitten the salt sea.

335

We must not surrender our souls
to adversity. We'll accomplish
nothing by being vexed,
O Bykchis. The best of drugs
is to fetch wine and get drunk.

336

A hurricane carried off his wits—
completely.

338

Zeus rains. Out of the sky
comes an enormous storm. Rivers
are frozen fast. Cast down

the storm. Lay on the fire. Mix
the sweet wine unsparingly.
Bind the soft wool to your brow.

342

Plant no tree
sooner than you do
the vine.

343

Nymphs, they say, are fashioned
by aegis-bearing Zeus.

344

This I know for sure: if a man moves gravel,
stone that's not securely workable,
the likelihood is he'll have a sore head.

345

What are these birds come from Ocean at the limits of earth,
these long-winged wild ducks with the dappled necks?

346

Let's drink! Why wait for the lamps?
There's only a finger of daylight left.
Hand down the big chased cups.
For Semele and the son of Zeus
gave wine to men to let them forget
their grief. So mix them one to two,
fill them right to the brim, and let
one cup thrust aside the next!

347

Now wet your throat with wine, for the star is circling round.
The summer season is hard. Everything thirsts from the heat.
In the leaves the cicada sings sweetly, and from under his wings
pours forth his long shrill song. The artichoke blooms.
Now women lust, but their men are too weak, because
the Dog Star parches them—head and knees and all.

348

They made that bastard Pittakos tyrant
of this lily-livered luckless city
and now in throngs they praise him to the skies.

350a

You have come from the ends of the earth having
the haft of your sword ivory bound with gold.

350b

A mighty labor, you saved them from grief,
slaying a warrior man who lacked
but one palm's breadth in height of five
royal cubits . . .

355

between the earth and the snowy sky

358

If wine shackles his wits,
he's not to be pursued;
he holds his head down
and blames his own soul
over and over again
and he regrets what he said—
but that's beyond recall.

359

child of rock and hoar sea

you puff up
children's hearts with pride,
you limpet of the sea.

360

Once, Aristodemos, they say,
at Sparta said a clever thing:
"Money's the man. No one poor
is either noble or in honor held."

362

Let someone put plaited garlands of dill
around my neck, sweet myrrh on my breast.

364

Poverty, cruel and irresistible ill,
with her sister Helplessness,
overcomes a great people.

365

A mighty stone, Aisimidas,
hangs over Tantalos' head.

366

Wine, dear boy, and truth

367

I heard the blossoming springtime coming.
Be quick and mix a bowl of the honey-sweet.

368

I bid you invite the charming Menon
if I'm to delight in the drinking bout.

369

drawing now from the honey-sweet,
now from wine more bitter than thistles

374

Welcome me,
the reveler,
welcome me,
I beg, I beg.

376

You drink goblets down,
sitting next to Dinnomenes.

380

I fell at the hands
of the Kypros-born.

383

Do the weapons of Dinnomenes,
the Tyrrhakean, glitter still
in the building called Myrsineon?

384

Sweetly smiling, sacred Sappho
of the violet-black braids

390

Women's blood is shed.

438

painting a lion from the sight of its claw

446

bites of cucumber

FRAGMENTS FROM SAPPHO OR ALKAIOS

11

taught Hero of Gyaros, that
girl of the quick-running feet

16

So harmoniously did Cretan women once
about the lovely altar dance with tender feet,

treading delicately upon
the tender bloom of the grass.

17

Such the lad who came to Thebes,
riding upon a chariot.

Malis was spinning
upon the spindle
a delicate linen thread.

25

I have flown to you
like a child to its mother.

ANAKREON

346, fr. 1

You have timorous wits as well,
boy of the beautiful face,

and your mother supposes that she
cleverly keeps you at home,
cherishingly,

but you have escaped
to fields of hyacinth
where Kypris tethered her steeds
freed from their straps.
Darting down to their midst,
you fluttered the hearts
of many a citizen.

Herotima, you public thoroughfare,
you public thoroughfare

346, fr. 4

I boxed with a harsh opponent,
but now I look up, I raise my head,
and owe great thanks that I
have escaped in every respect
the bonds of Love
Aphrodite made tough.
Let someone bring wine in a jar
and water that bubbles.

347

of the hair that shadowed
your delicate neck.

But now you are bald. Your hair
has fallen into squalid hands
and dropped all of a heap
to the dark dust below

at the wretched iron's stroke.
But I am worn away with anguish.
What is one to do who cannot
succeed even for Thrace?

I hear the notorious woman
thinks pitiable thoughts
and often says things like this
as she blames her destiny:

You'd do me a favor, mother,
if you'd carry and cast me away
into the pitiless sea that boils,
billowing purple-black.

348

I beseech you, huntress of deer,
tawny-haired daughter of Zeus,
queen of wild beasts, who now
beside swirling Lethaios behold
a city of bold-hearted men and rejoice
that you shepherd citizens not untamed.

349

Look, this man flouts
the soldiers of Ialysos
with their dark blue shields.

351

Mischievous men fight
with the keeper of the door.

352

That cheerful fellow Megistes for ten months now
has worn a crown of osier and drunk the honey must.

353

On the island, Megistes,
rebellious fishermen
control the town.

354

Among my neighbors
you will make me
of ill report.

356a

Come, boy, bring me a bowl
that I may drink a long draft.
Pour ten cups of water and five
of wine that I may once again
become a Bacchant, not boisterously.

356b

Come, again, let us no longer
with clatter and uproar over our wine
practice the drinking of Skyths but imbibe,
with lovely songs, moderately.

357

O lord, with whom subduing Love
and the dark-eyed nymphs
    and rosy Aphrodite
play, as you stroll the lofty mountain peaks,

I beseech you, propitiously
come to me and hear my prayer
    and find it pleasing:
Counsel Kleoboulos well, Dionysos,
    that he accept my love.

358

Once more the golden-haired god
tosses his purple ball,
invites me to play with the girl
who wears the spangled shoe.
But she, for she's from well-
built Lesbos, scoffs
at my graying hair and gapes
after another girl.

359

I'm in love with Kleoboulos.
I'm mad for Kleoboulos.
I'm agog at Kleoboulos.

360

Boy, with the look of a girl,
I pursue you, but you care not,
for you know not that you
are the charioteer of my soul.

361

I'd not wish
for Amalthea's horn
nor to be the king
of Tartessos for
the length of a hundred
and fifty years.

363

Why do you fly
to anoint with myrrh
a chest more hollow than pipes?

364

for Targelios says that you
throw the discus gracefully.

365

many times, Dionysos,
loud roaring

366

O Smerdis, thrice swept out

367

for you were unbending toward me

368

for Leukippe you're in a whirl

370

and not my tender sister

372

Artemon, that litter rider,
attracts Eurypyle the blond.

373

For supper I had a small piece of bread,
and I drank down a whole keg of wine.
Now, delicately, I pluck my lovely lute
and make serenade to that dear girl Poliarche.

374

Holding the magadis,
I twang its twenty strings
while you, Leukaspis,
exult in your youth.

375

Who has turned his soul
to lovely youth and dances to
the tender half-bored flutes?

376

Once again from high upon
the Leukadian cliff I dive
into the foaming wave,
drunk with love.

377

The Mysians discovered the mating
of asses mounting mares.

378

I flutter up to Olympos
on nimble wings,
looking for Love,

for my boy doesn't want
to be young with me.

380

Hail, dear light, with a charming smile upon your face.

383

The handmaiden held
the three-ladle bowl
and poured the wine,
honey-sweet.

384

And not yet then
did Persuasion shine,
silvery.

385

I come up from the river
and bring everything
shining bright.

386

Simalos I saw in the choral dance,
and he was holding his lovely lyre.

387

I asked Strattis, the perfume maker,
if he would let his hair grow long.

388

Before, he went around in rags, a wasped cap,
with knucklebones of wood in his ears and about his ribs
the hairless hide of an ox,
the wrap of a cheap shield, that scoundrel Artemon,
who consorted with bread-selling women and willing whores,
        and scraped
a spurious living. Often
his neck was in the stocks, often upon the wheel.
Often his back was flogged with a leather whip, his hair
and beard plucked out. But now
the son of Kyke rides upon a chariot,
wears earrings of gold, and carries an ivory parasol,
exactly as the ladies do.

389

To strangers you're a friendly girl,
so let me, thirsting, drink.

390

The lovely-haired daughters of Zeus lightly danced.

391

But now the city's crown has been destroyed.

393

Ares, eager for the fray,
loves a man staunch with the spear.

394a

The swallow, graceful and melodious

394b

Once again bald Alexis goes a-courting.

395

Already my temples are hoar
and my head white, and I
no longer have the grace
of youth. My teeth are old.
Not much time is left
of sweet life now, and so
often I sob in dread
of Tartaros. For terrible
is Hades' cove and awful
the road down, for certain
it is that he who descends
does not come up again.

396

Bring water, boy, bring wine,
and bring me flowering crowns.
Bring them that I may box with Love.

397

They put about their breasts
woven garlands of lotus buds.

398

The knucklebones of Love
are madness and uproar.

399

She took off her dress
to be a Dorian girl.

400

Again I went down
to Pythomander's house,
escaping from Love.

402a

I'd love to play with you,
you have such a charming way.

402c

Children love me for my lines,
for I sing charming songs and know
how to say charming words as well.

403

I am borne over reefs unseen.

407

But pledge me, dear boy, your delicate thighs.

408

soft-eyed as a young
suckling fawn, afraid
when his horned mother
abandons him in a wood

410

Let's put little wreaths of parsley upon our brows
and keep a holiday feast for Dionysos the god.

411a

May it be mine to die,
for there could be
no other release
from these sorrows of mine.

411b

Dionysos' swaying Bassarids

412

Won't you let me,
now that I'm drunk,
go off home?

413

Love, like a smith,
struck me with a mighty ax,
then doused me in a wintry
mountain stream.

414

You've cut off a blameless blossom of soft hair.

416

I hate
all those with their subtle, demanding

ways. I've learned that you, Megistes,
are one of the innocents.

417

Thracian filly, why do you look at me askance
and flee me so relentlessly? Do you think that I
know nothing at all? Be sure that I could bridle you,
put on the reins, and take you round the course's end.
But now you graze the meadow, play in your skittish way.
That's just because you have no rider to break you.

418

Listen to an old man,
girl with the pretty hair
and the yellow dress.

419

O Aristokleides,
I pity you first
of my stouthearted friends,
for you wasted your youth
warding slavery off
from your native land.

420

when white hairs mingle with my black

421

My wits are struck dumb.

422

shaking your Thracian hair

423 a and b

Zeus, put to sleep solecian speech
lest you babble barbarously.

425

You are like gentle guests.
You need only fire
and a roof overhead.

426

Once long ago Milesians
were stouthearted men.

427

Don't babble like the sea's
billow, swilling down
with cunning Gastrodora
the cup drunk at the hearth.

428

I love, and again I don't.
I'm mad, and again I'm not.

429

If he wants to fight,
let him fight,
for it is allowed.

430

You're too enthusiastic.

431

Although he does not shoot
the bolt on his double doors,
he sleeps peacefully.

432

Now I am wrinkled,
overripe, because
of your lustfulness.

433

I had a full cup
and drank it down
to Erxion
of the white crest.

434

Each man had garlands three,
two of roses, one of Naukratis.

435

spread with all kinds of good things

436

to put your hand in the frying pan

437

I fled from her
like the cuckoo bird.

439

twining thighs about thighs

440

You are attractive
to far too many.

441

a. He chopped through
the middle of the neck

b. and the robe was split
straight down.

443

Among the black-leaved laurel
and the pale-green olive
he sways.

445

Bullies and reckless you are,
nor do you know at whom
you'll whirl your weapons.

447

sea-purple dye

452

parading about with arched neck

453

a babbling swallow

456

slender colts

458

stepping effeminately

505d

I'm eager to sing of delicate Love
who luxuriates in abundantly
blossoming wreaths. He's potentate
of gods and masters mortals too.

Elegiac Fragments

1

It doesn't please your heart at all. Nevertheless,
I wait for you without any doubt at all.

2

I do not love the man who beside the full
mixing bowl drinks his wine and talks
of quarrels and tearful war. I love the man who
mingles the glorious gifts of Aphrodite
with those of the Muses and remembers the lovely feast.

SIMONIDES

506

Who of those alive
has bound himself about
with so many myrtle leaves
or garlands of roses, because
he has won in a contest of those
who are dwellers-about?

507

Not scantily was shorn
the Ram when he entered upon
the shining precinct of Zeus
with all its splendor of trees.

508

Just as when Zeus admonishes
in the month of wintry storms
the fourteen days that fall
before the solstice and after,
called by mortal men
the sacred, windless time
when the pied halcyon
nourishes her young

509

Neither Polydeukes' might
nor Alkmena's iron son
would have lifted fists
against him.

512

Drink, drink, for fortune's favor!

514

pursuing an octopus

515

Hail, O daughters of storm-fleet steeds!

516

The dust at the wheel
rose with the drift
of the wind.

517

lest he let go from his hands
the crimson-colored reins

520

Slight the strength of men
and useless their cares.
In a short life
toil upon toil.
Inescapable death
hovers nevertheless.
The noble and base
have got by lot
the same share of that.

521

Being mortal, never say what tomorrow
will bring, nor seeing a man blest,
how long he will be, for change
is as swift as the turn
of a dragonfly's wing.

522

Everything comes to the same
frightful Charybdis,
great valor and also wealth.

523

Not even those who existed before
and were born half-immortal from
the lord gods arrived at old age
completing a life without pain,
without risk, imperishable.

524

Death overtakes even the man
who on battle turns his back.

525

Easily do the gods
cheat the mind of man.

526

No one without the gods
acquires excellence, neither city nor
mortal man. The contriver of all is god.
Among men nothing without toil.

527

There is no evil that man
cannot expect. In just a little time
god turns all upside down.

531

To those who fell at Thermopylai
belongs a glorious fate, a noble destiny.
An altar their tomb; in place of lamentation,
memory; for pity, praise.
Entombment like this neither mold
nor time that masters all shall dim.
This sepulcher of noble men has taken
as its attendant the good repute of Hellas.
Leonidas, the Spartan king, gives witness
of this: he left behind a mighty ornament
of valor and glory everlasting.

533a

there boomed of the sea

533b

They turned away the winged Deaths.

536

who lyrically on Salamis

538

Every lark must sprout a crest.

542

It is hard to become a truly good man,
fashioned foursquare, without fault,
  in hand and foot and mind,

nor does Pittakos' maxim harmonize
with mine, although spoken by a wise man.
  He said, "Hard to be good."
God alone could have this prize. A man
  cannot not be bad
if hopeless disaster crushes him, for while
he's fortunate, any man is good,
but bad when his luck is bad.

Therefore never would I cast away
my portion of life in pursuit of the not-to-be
  for an empty, impracticable hope:
a blameless man among those who reap the fruit
  of the broad-foundationed earth.
But if I discover him, I'll send you word.
All those I praise and love who willingly
do nothing disgraceful. Not even the gods fight
with necessity . . .

. . . not too lawless
and knowing justice to benefit a city,
a healthy man. I'll never find fault,
Of the worthless the generations are countless.
Surely, unmixed with evil, all is fair.

543

When on the carved chest
the wind blew,
and the rolling sea brought
fear with its crash,
her cheek wet, she put
her arm around Perseus
and said, "O child,
what trouble I have,

but you sleep, slumber
your suckling way,
laid in the black,
brass-nailed bark,
in the blue mist
of dark. You know not
the brine, deep on your hair,
from the passing wave,
nor the voice of the wind,
while you lie
in your purple robe,
my pretty babe.
If this danger
were danger to you,
you'd give your delicate ear
to my word. But now I say,
sleep my babe,
let the sea sleep,
sleep our measureless woe.
May some change come,
father Zeus, from you.
Where my prayer is too bold,
beyond what is right,
forgive me."

550a

a crimson sail drenched
in the pliant bloom
of the flourishing
evergreen oak

551

Had I got here sooner,
I'd have given you a boon
greater than life.

553

They wept for the suckling child
of the violet-wreathed girl as he
breathed his sweet life away.

555

Hermes grants it well,
god of the games, child
of glancing-eyed Maia
who haunts the mountaintops,
whom Atlas begat, exceeding
in beauty his seven daughters
of violet locks, dear
to him, and whom men call
the heavenly Pleiades.

559

Be gracious, mother
of twenty young.

564

who with the spear
conquered all the youths, casting
across the swirling Anauros
from Iolkos of many clusters
of grapes, for so Stesichorus
and Homer sang to the peoples

567

There fluttered above his head
countless birds, and fish
at his lovely song leapt
straight out of the dark blue sea.

571

The noise of the purple roiling sea
surrounds and holds me fast.

575

Wretched child of wile-devising Aphrodite,
whom she bore to wile-contriving Ares

577a

Where for purification is drawn
the sacred water from beneath
the home of the Muses of lovely hair

577b

Overseer of holy lustration waters

579

The story is
that valor dwells upon
inaccessible rocks . . .
and haunts a holy place,
nor do mortal eyes behold her,
unless sweat that eats the soul
comes from within and a man reaches
the very peak of bravery.

581

Who with any sense would praise
Kleoboulos, inhabitant of Lindos,
who opposed the might of a gravestone
to eternally running river streams,
the blossoms of spring, the blaze of the sun

and golden moon, the swirls of the sea?
All these are less than the gods. A stone
even mortal hands can break.
This is the plan of a foolish man.

583

cock of clarion call

584

What mortal life
apart from pleasure
could one desire?
What tyranny?
Apart from this
not even the life
of the gods is to be
envied at all.

585

From her rosy mouth
the maid let fall her voice.

586

When in the spring
from throbbing throats
the warbling nightingales

587

Fire the wild beasts
hated most of all.

590

In times of necessity
even the harsh is sweet.

592

a. at hand refined gold

b. pure, without lead

593

making tawny-colored honey

594

sinks last beneath the earth

595

nor was there then
so much as a breath
of wind to rustle the leaves
and keep the spreading
honey-sweet voice
from reaching mortal ears.

597

glorious messenger
of sweet-scented spring,
the dark blue swallow

598

Seeming forces even the truth.

599

but this one, possessed of sweet sleep

600

a breeze that stipples the sea

602

New wine does not
yet refute the gift
of last year's vine.
The tale of empty-
headed youths.

603

For what has come about
will never be undone.

605

only the sun in the sky

612

wind-cherished gates

618

bond women working the wool

625

blue-prowed

630

blackly dark

631

eared cup

636

a three-barbed arrow

638

a repelling stench

639

how I laughs

KORINNA

654

"The Kouretes hid the goddess'
very holy infant
in a cave. They kept the secret
from Kronos of crooked counsel
that time that divine Rhea
deceived him and got
great honor from the gods."
That is what he sang.
Straightway the Muses
bade the blessed ones
put their secret ballot
stones in golden urns.
They all rose up together.
Kithairon got the more.
Straightway Hermes
called out that he had got
the lovely victory.
The blessed ones crowned him
with garlands. His heart was glad.
But Helikon was crushed
by bitter grief. He tore
loose a smooth rock.
The mountain gave way.
Crying piteously,
he hurled it straight down
into countless stones.

. . . .

Of your daughters, three
Zeus, king and father
of all, has as brides.
Three Poseidon, lord
of the sea, has wed, and two

Phoibos has taken to bed,
and one the noble son
of Maia, Hermes, has.
For so Kypris and Eros
persuaded them to go
secretly to your house
and take your daughters nine.
They in time will bear
a race of demigods
and be fruitful and ageless,
and from the oracular tripod

. . . .

this honor . . .
from fifty mighty kinsmen
I, a preeminent prophet,
Akraiphen, obtained the truth
from the sacred sanctuary.
For first the son of Leto
gave to Euonymos
from his own tripods the right
to proclaim oracles.
Him Hyrieus cast
from out the land and got
that honor after him.
He was Poseidon's son.
Next Orion, my sire,
regained his land for himself
and strolls the heavens now.
This is the honor . . .
Therefore, I speak the truth
oracular, and do you
yield to immortal gods
and set your mind at rest,
a father-in-law to gods.
So spoke the holy seer,
and Asopos gladly clasped
his right hand and shed
from his eye a tear and said

. . . .

664a

And I, I find fault
with tuneful Myrtis, because,
being a woman, once
she strove against Pindar.

PRAXILLA

747

The loveliest thing I leave is the light of the sun,
then the shining stars and the face of the moon
and ripe cucumbers and apples and pears.

748

But they never persuaded the heart in your breast.

749

Learn the tale of Admetos, my friend,
    and cultivate the brave.
Despise the company of cowards. There's
    little favor from them.

750

Beware, my friend, beneath every stone a scorpion.

754

looking so prettily through the window,
a virgin above, but all woman below

ANONYMOUS

892

As the crab said when he got
the snake in his claw, "You must
be a straight friend and not
think with crooked thoughts."

893

I'll bear my sword in a myrtle bough
like Harmodios and Aristogeiton
when they slew the tyrant and made
Athens a democracy.

894

Dearest Harmodios, you're not
really dead. They say you live
in the islands of the blest, where
Achilles, swift of foot, dwells
and Diomedes, Tydeus' son.

895

I'll bear my sword in a myrtle bough
like Harmodios and Aristogeiton
when at Athena's feast they slew
that fellow Hipparchos, the tyrant man.

896

Your glory will last forever throughout
the land, dearest Harmodios

and Aristogeiton, because you slew
the tyrant, making Athens free.

899

Spearman Ajax, son of Telamon,
you were noblest of the Danaans,
they say, after Achilles, to come to Troy.

900

Would that I were a lovely ivory lyre
and that lovely lads would carry me
to choruses sung and danced for Dionysos.

901

Would that I were a beautiful gaud
of unrefined gold and that a beautiful woman
might wear me, making her mind pure.

848

The swallow has come, has come.
She brings the lovely seasons,
she brings the lovely years.
Her belly is white and black
her back. From your fatted house
roll forth your fruited cake,
your little goblet of wine,
your wicker basket of cheese.
Bread of wheat or pulse
the swallow refuses not.
Are we to get or go?
We'll go if we get. If not,
you'll not get off. We'll take
the lintel and door and wife

who sits inside. She's small.
We'll easily carry her off.
If you've got little to give,
may you get something big.
To the swallow, open, open
the door, for we are not
old men but children yet.

852

Where are my roses? Where are my violets?
　　Where is my pretty parsley?
Here are your roses. Here are your violets.
　　Here is your pretty parsley.

869

Grind, mill, grind,
for even Pittakos ground,
tyrant of great Mytilene.

902

Drink, be young, love, wear wreaths with me.
Be mad when I am mad and sober when I am.

904

The pig has her acorn, the one she wants to have,
and I my pretty girl, the one I want to have.

S 458

A spangle of stars
in the dark blue night

BAKCHYLIDES

Epinician III

For Hiero of Syracuse
Victor in the Four-Horse Chariot Race at Olympia, 468 B.C.

Sing of Demeter, mistress
    of Sicily, gloriously
fruited, and of her Daughter,
    wreathed in violets,
Klio of sweet gifts,
    and then of Hiero's horses
that coursed at Olympia.
    For with Glory and Victory
preeminent they sped
    beside the wide swirls
of Alpheus, and there they assured
    Deinomenes' blessed son
the achievement of garlands. The people
    shouted out . . .
The thrice fortunate man,
    who held by Zeus' lot
the honor to rule Greeks
    in number more than any
other, had the wit
    not to shroud in cloak
of dark towered wealth.
    His sanctuaries teem
with festal sacrifice
    of oxen. His streets brim
with hospitality.
    Gold sparkles and gleams
from high and gorgeously wrought
    tripods set before
the shrines where Delphians tend
    Phoibos' greatest grove
beside Kastalia's streams.
    Let us glorify the god,

22–50 the god, for that is best
of all prosperities.
For once when Zeus had fulfilled
his fated destiny,
and Sardis had been sacked
by the Persian host, Apollo
of the golden sword saved
Kroisos, the king of horse-
taming Lydia. He,
when he approached the day,
unforeseen and filled
with tears, chose not to endure
for a moment slavery
but had built a pyre
before the brazen-walled court,
and there with his honored wife
and lovely-haired daughters,
who wept insatiably,
he stepped upon the pile.
Casting up his hands
to the steep heaven he called,
"Powerful deity,
where now is the grace of gods?
Where is the lord, son
of Leto? Alyattes' house
falls to ruin . . .
. . . myriad . . .
. . . city . . .
gold-swirling Paktolos
blushes red with blood.
Women, disreputably,
are led from well-built halls.
What was hateful before is dear;
the sweetest of all to die."
So much he said and bade
the softly stepping slave
kindle the structure of wood.
His maiden daughters shrieked
and cast their dear hands

to their mother. Death foreseen 51–79
is the worst slaughter of all.
But when the flashing force
of the horrible flame leapt,
then Zeus sent a black-
cloaking cloud to quench
the red-orange blaze.
Nothing is past belief
when fashioned by gods' concern.
Then Delian Apollo
carried the old man
to the land of Hyperboreans
and settled him there together
with his delicate-ankled daughters
because of his piety,
for he had sent to Pytho,
that very sacred shrine,
greater gifts than any
other mortal man.
No one of those who dwell
in Hellas will dare to say
that any mortal man
has sent more gold than you,
O Hiero, greatly praised,
to Loxias. One may speak
well of him who battens
not on envy . . .
a horse-loving warrior man
who has the scepter of Zeus
and a share of the violet-haired
Muses . . .
. . . ephemeral
you see. Life is short.
Winged is the hope of creatures
of a day. The lord Apollo
said to Pheres' son,
"A mortal man must nourish
double thoughts, that he
will see only tomorrow's

80–91 sun or will complete
a life of fifty years
deep in wealth. Doing
holy deeds, cheer
your heart, for this is best
of rewards." I speak to those
who understand. The deep
ether is undefiled.
The sea's water does not
rot. Gold is delight.
A man is not permitted
to pass by hoary age
and then recover again
his blossoming youth. The light
of excellence diminishes
not with mortal flesh.
The Muse nourishes it.
Hiero, you have shown
to mortals the loveliest blossoms
of wealth. Silence does not
become a prosperous man.
With truth of loveliness
someone will sing
the grace of the honey-tongued
Kean nightingale.

Epinician V

For Hiero of Syracuse
Victor in the Horse Race at Olympia, 476 B.C.

Warlord, blessed by fate,
    of the Syracusans whirled
in chariots, you will know
    the sweet-gifted glory
of Muses, violet crowned,
    if any do of those
now upon earth,
    and rightly. Give your mind
of straight judgment relief
    from care and gaze in thought
at this: whether it was
    with the full-breasted Graces your guest
wove a hymn and sent it
    from his hallowed isle
to your famed city, a glorious
    attendant of Heaven who wears
the golden diadem.
    He wishes to pour voice
from his chest in praise of Hiero.
    Cleaving the deep ether,
the eagle with swift wings,
    messenger of wide-
ruling, loud-roaring Zeus,
    trusts in his mighty strength
and takes heart, and the shrill-
    piping birds cower
in fear. Neither peaks
    of the huge earth, nor steep
waves of unwearying sea
    impede him. In unabating
void he plies with breath
    of the west wind his plumage,

27–60 a gloss of feathers and down,
conspicuous to see.
So now also for me
myriad are the paths
to sing your excellence
for the sake of Victory
of the blue-black hair
and brazen-breasted Ares,
noble children of
Deinomenes. May god
never weary of favoring you.
Dawn of the golden arms
beheld Pherenikos,
the storm-swift bay colt,
victorious beside
the wide-eddying Alpheus
and at very holy Pytho.
I call upon Earth to witness:
no dust in the race from horses
ahead befouled him
as he achieved the goal.
Like a blast of the north wind,
sensitive to his pilot,
he sped to a victory
that met with fresh applause
for Hiero, generous to guests.
Blessed is he to whom
god grants a share of goods
and with enviable chance a life
of wealth. For no one of those
upon this earth is blessed
in every respect. Once,
they say, that irresistible
breaker of gates, the sprig
of Zeus who flashes light
from his thunderbolt, went down
to slender-ankled Persephone's
house to bring to the light
from Hades the jag-toothed hound,

implacable Echidna's son.
There he knew the souls
of wretched mortals beside
Kokytos' streams, as many
as the leaves that the wind shakes
on Ida's shining shoulders,
and among them the shade
of the stouthearted shaker of spears,
Meleager, son of Porthaon,
whom that wondrous hero,
Alkmena's son, saw
gleaming bright in arms.
He fixed the twanging string
to the arch of his bow and then,
lifting his quiver's lid,
took an arrow tipped with bronze.
Meleager's ghost appeared
opposite him and said,
knowing him well, this:
"Son of mighty Zeus,
stand where you are. Calm
your soul and speed not
in vain at perished shades
your swift shaft from your hands.
There is no need to fear."
So he spoke, and the lord,
the son of Amphitryon,
marveled and said to him,
"Who of immortal men
or even of mortals reared
a shoot like this? Upon
what sort of earth? And who
slew him? Perhaps
Hera, beautifully sashed,
will dispatch that man against
my head. But blond Pallas,
no doubt, will concern herself
with matters like these."
But Meleager wept

93–123/125 and addressed him so:
"It is difficult for men
upon the earth to avert
the purpose of the gods.
Otherwise would Oineus,
my father, driver of steeds,
have stayed with sacrifice
of many goats and oxen
with ruddy backs the wrath
of holy Artemis, wreathed
in buds, of ivory arms,
but unconquerable was
the goddess's wrath. She sped
a boar, broad in strength,
shameless in battle, against
Kalydon of the lovely
dancing grounds, where
with might of floods he sheared
with his tusk the vine rows
and slaughtered flocks and men
who came opposite him.
The noblest of us Greeks
did loathsome battle against
the boar, sedulously,
for six consecutive days.
When fate gave mastery
to us Aitolians,
we buried those whom
the bellowing boar had slain
in the rushing force of attack,
Ankaios and Agelaos,
the best of my honored brothers,
whom Althaia bore in the halls,
famed afar, of Oineus.
A delightful destiny,
for never did
Leto's savage daughter,
her mind intent on war,
leave off her wrath. We raged,

intent for the tawny hide,
with Kouretes, staunch in the fray.
Then I with many another
slew Iphikles and noble
Aphares, my mother's brothers,
for Ares, hard of heart,
does not distinguish a friend
in war, but blindly the shafts
are launched against the souls
of foes and bear death
to whomever the god wills.
Taking no account
of this, the cunning daughter
of Thestios, my mother,
of evil destiny,
a fearless woman, plotted
destruction for me. She took
from the carved chest the log
of my brief destiny
and kindled it. Fate
had allotted it to be
the boundary stone of life
for me. I was about
to slay Klymenos,
Daïpylos' valiant son,
blameless of form, before
the battlements, for they fled
toward the ancient citadel,
sturdily built, of Pleuron,
when my sweet soul failed,
my strength diminished—alas!—
and breathing my last, I wept,
poor wretch, at leaving behind
my glorious youth." They say
that then alone did the child
of Amphitryon, who did
not fear the battle cry,
wet with tears his eyes
in pity for the destiny

159–191 of the wretchedly suffering man,
and answering him he said,
"Best for mortals not
to be born nor to look upon
the light of the sun. It is
no use to weep for this,
but one must speak of that
that can come to accomplishment.
Is there in the halls
of war-loving Oineus some
unmarried daughter like you
in form? Gladly would I
make her my shining bride."
The shade of Meleager,
steadfast in battle, replied,
"I left behind in my house
tender-necked Deianeira,
unknowing yet of the charms
of seductive Aphrodite."
O, Kalliope of
the ivory arms, stay
your chariot, beautifully made,
just here, and sing of Zeus,
Kronos' son, Olympian king
of gods, and Alpheus of
unwearying flood, and Pelops,
and Pisa, where the famed
Pherenikos galloped the course,
victorious, and brought
to the city of Syracuse
of beautiful battlements
for Hiero the olive leaf
of happiness. One must
give praise for the sake of truth
and thrust envy away
with both our hands if one
of mortals fares well.
A Boiotian man said this,

Hesiod, of the sweet 192–197
Graces the minister:
"Whom immortals honor
mortals' fame attends."
Easily am I
persuaded to send to Hiero
a tongue . . . from the path.
For thence do the stocks of good
flourish and bloom. May Zeus,
the greatest father, preserve
them undisturbed in peace.

Epinician XIII

For Pytheas of Aigina
Victor in the Pankration at Nemea, 481 B.C.(?)

. . . .

He will put a stop
to their arrogant violence,
ordaining justice for men.
What a heavy hand
with manifold skills the scion
of Perseus casts upon
the carnivorous lion,
for the glittering man-slaying bronze
will not penetrate
that unassailable flesh.
The sword is bent back.
Surely sometime, I say,
there will be here for wreaths
the sweat and toil of Greeks
in the pankration.
For this, beside the altar
of prime-ruling Zeus,
blossoms of Victory,
bringing glory for those
few of mortals wreathed
with them, nourish forever
famed reputation of gold
for all the time that they live,
and whenever the blue-black cloud
of death cloaks them over,
immortal glory is left
of the deed well done, and with
a destiny secure.
Such you chanced upon
at Nemea, Lampon's son,

your hair crowned with wreaths
of every blossoming bud,
. . . city of steep streets
. . . revelers' songs
. . . of sweet breath
. . . delighting mortals
to your ancestral isle
you come displaying your strength,
tremendous and triumphant.
O daughter of swirling river,
Aigina of gentle intent,
surely the son of Kronos
has given great honor
to you in every game
and shone you as a beacon
torch to all the Greeks.
And some exultant girl
with fluttering feet
like a frivolous fawn will leap
along the flowering banks,
nimbly, with glorious friends
of familiar companionship.
And girls, garlanded,
in native play, with reed
and crimson buds, sing
and dance, O queen,
. . . of this welcoming land
and Endaïs of rosy
arms, who bore Peleus
and mighty Telamon,
lying with Aiakos
as consort in bed of love.
Their battle-arousing sons,
Achilles the swift and the child
of lovely Eriboia,
Ajax, the spirited shield-
bearing hero, I'll sing,
who, staunch at the prow,

withstood the bold-hearted Hektor,
  brazen corsleted,
as he rushed the Greek ships
  with ineffable flame
when the son of Peleus stirred
  his implacable anger against
the sons of Atreus and so
  delayed the Dardanians' doom.
They had not before
  left Ilion's wondrous,
turreted citadel
  but cowered, distraught with fear
at the fierce battle, as long
  as Achilles, confoundingly,
raged in the plain below,
  shaking his murderous spear.
But when he abandoned the war,
  that dauntless son of Thetis,
the Nereid, violet crowned,
  just as in the black-
blossoming sea Boreas
  cleaves men's hearts beneath
the billows as night comes on
  but leaves off when Dawn
brings light to mortal men
  and a breeze smoothes the sea—
they belly their sail with breath
  of the South Wind and reach
happily the shore
  they never hoped to see—
so the Trojans, when
  they heard that the spearman
Achilles lingered at
  the tents because of the blond
Briseis of lovely limbs,
  stretched their hands to the gods,
seeing the gleaming sun
  beneath the wintry storm.
With all speed they left

Laomedon's walls and leapt
into the plain and bore
with them ferocious strife.
In the Danaans they roused
terror and Ares, well-lanced,
and Loxias Apollo, lord
of the Lykians, drove them on,
and they reached the shore of the sea.
Beside the beautifully sterned
ships they battled and the earth
reddened with gore of men
slain at Hektor's hand.

. . . .

Not in the lampless dark
of night is shining valor
hidden, but brimming with fame,
secure, she strolls the land
and the ever-rolling sea.
She honors the glorifying
isle of Aiakos,
and with garland-loving fame
she pilots this city and with
prudent government,
who has the feast as her lot,
and she keeps the cities in peace
of goodly god-fearing men.
The glorious victory, youths,
of Pytheas sing and the care
of Menander, his trainer, as well,
which at Alpheus' streams
often august Athena
of golden chariot
has honored with high heart
and crowned with fillets the locks
of myriad men in the games
of All the Gathered Greeks.
Let him who is not constrained
by envy of audacious speech

201–220 praise a man of skill,
justly. Censure of men
accrues to every deed,
but truth is wont to win,
and all-subduing time
will always augment the fame
of a work well done. His foes' . . .
idle tongues diminish . . .
unseen . . .

. . . .

cheers his heart with hope,
and I, trusting in that,
and to the Muses of crimson
diadems, now show
this new-woven gift of songs
and honor the splendorous
hospitality
which Lampon [offered me]
expecting nothing mean,
and if in truth Klio,
all blossoming, has distilled
these in my heart, then songs
with words delighting the soul
will herald him to all.

Dithyramb XVI

since
Ourania, beautifully throned,
has sent to me a bark
of gold, brimming with hymns,
famed afar . . .

. . . . . .

whether he rejoices
beside the foaming Hebros
or takes his heart's delight
in the long-necked swan
. . . you come in quest
of Paian blossoms of song,
Pythian Apollo,
all those the choruses
at Delphi make ring
beside your glorious shrine
before we celebrate
how Amphitryon's son,
a mortal bold in design,
abandoned Oichalia,
devoured by fire, and came
to a shore the waves washed around.
There he sacrificed
from his spoil to Kenaian Zeus
of the wide clouds nine
deep-bellowing bulls,
and two to Poseidon who
agitates the sea
and devastates the land,
and to virgin Athena, whose glance
quells, an unyoked ox
of high horns. And then
an irresistible demon
wove for Deianeira

24–35 a shrewd device, all tears,
when she heard the heartbreaking news
that the son of Zeus, dauntless
in battle, was sending on
Iole of snowy arms
to his splendid house to be
his bride. How tragic, ill-starred
that she contrived device
like this. For jealousy,
so spreading in strength, destroyed
her and the murky veil
of what was afterward
to come when upon
Lykormos' rosy bank
she accepted from Nessos the centaur
the fiendish portentous gift.

Dithyramb XVII

The ship with indigo prow
    that bore Theseus steadfast
in the battle clash together
    with twice seven splendid
Ionian lads and girls
    cut the Cretan main,
for upon the sail that gleamed
    from afar there fell the breeze
of Boreas by grace
    of glorious Athena
who shakes her goatskin cape.
    The hallowed gifts of Kypris,
goddess wreathed with desire,
    pricked at Minos' heart,
and he no longer withheld
    his hand from a girl but touched
her snowy translucent cheek.
    Eriboia shouted aloud
to Pandion's seed who wore
    a corselet of bronze.
Theseus saw. Beneath
    his brow his eye rolled
black, and a wracking pain
    tore at his heart. He spoke:
"Son of peerless Zeus,
    no longer do you steer
a spirit within your wit
    righteously. Restrain,
hero, presumptuous
    violence. Whatever
fate destiny nods
    for us from above, weighting
the scale of Zeus, we will
    fulfill when the time comes.

28–59 Contain your offensive intent.
If the cherished girl of Phoinix,
she of the lovely name,
who lay in the bed of Zeus
beneath the brow of Ida
bore you the best of mortals,
nevertheless, the daughter
of rich Pittheus who lay
with lord Poseidon gave birth
to me when the violet-wreathed
Nereids presented her
with a wedding veil of gold.
And so I bid you,
warlord of Knossos,
check that lust, the cause
of many a moan to come.
I should not choose to see
the lovely immortal light
of Dawn should you subdue
against his will any
of these girls or boys.
First will I show the strength
of my hands, and god shall judge
the events that follow after."
So spoke the hero, skilled
in the spear, and the sailors marveled
at the magnificent boldness
of the man. The heart of Helios'
son-in-law was angered,
and he wove a strange plot
and spoke, "Mighty in strength,
Father Zeus, hear!
If Phoenix' daughter, she
of the lovely arms, bore me
to you, send forth now
from heaven the lightning bolt,
trailing in speed its tresses
of flame, a conspicuous sign,
and if Aithra of Troezen

bore you to Poseidon, the shaker
of earth, then fetch this gleaming
ring of gold from my hand
from out of the salt depths,
diving boldly down
to your father's ocean home.
So will you know if Kronos' son,
thunder-king and lord
of all, hears my prayer."
Zeus, mighty in strength,
heard the blameless prayer
and willingly begot
for Minos, his dear son,
preeminent honor, plain
for all to see; he sent
the lightning flash. The hero,
steadfast in battle clash,
beheld the pleasing portent
and spread his arms wide
to the blazing sky and said,
"Theseus, you see these gifts,
clearly mine from Zeus.
Dive, therefore, into
the roaring sea depth,
and Poseidon, Kronos' son,
will accomplish surpassing glory
for you throughout all the girth
of the beautifully wooded earth."
So he spoke. The soul
of Theseus did not recoil
but upon the well-stacked deck
he took his stand and leapt
and, willing, the precinct of sea
welcomed him. The son
of Zeus marveled within
his heart and bade them keep
the cunningly crafted bark
before the wind. But fate
prepared another course.

90–119 The ship sped swiftly on,
for the breath of Boreas
blew from behind and the tribe
of Athenian youths trembled
with fright when the hero leapt
into the depth and shed tears
down from their lily eyes,
accepting his destiny.
But dolphins, those seafaring beasts,
speedily bore enormous
Theseus to the house
of his father, lord of the horse.
He entered the halls of the gods.
He feared the glorious daughters
of fortunate Nereus there.
From their glistening limbs
there gleamed, as it were,
the beam of fire. Ribbons
braided with gold encircled
their locks. With lissome feet
they delighted their hearts in dance.
In that lovely house he saw
his father's majestic wife,
beloved Amphitrite
of the wide ox eyes.
She wrapped him round with a cloak
of purple, sea-dyed,
and on his springing hair
she placed the perfect wreath,
with roses shadowed dark,
that at her marriage feast
the clever Aphrodite
had bequeathed to her. To men
of sound wit nothing
the gods will passes
belief. Beside the ship
of slender stern Theseus
appeared. Alas, in what

thoughts did he entangle
    the Knossian captain when he
emerged dry from the deep,
    a marvel to all, for there shone
upon him the gods' gifts,
    and the girls of the gleaming thrones
shrilled with novel frivolity,
    and the sea resounded loud.
The youths nearby cried
    the paian with lovely voice.
Delian, cheer your heart
    with Kean dances and grant
happiness, god-sent.

Dithyramb XVIII

Theseus

King of sacred Athens,
    lord of the dainty-lived
Ionians, what novelty
    has the brazen-belled trumpet
rung out in its war song?
    Has some hostile general
beset the boundaries
    of our land with attack?
Do thieves of evil device
    in their shepherds' despite
drive off perforce our flocks
    of sheep? What lacerates
your heart? Please tell. For you,
    if any man, I think,
have help of sturdy youths,
    Pandion's son and Kreousa's.
A herald has just run
    the long Isthmian road.
He reports the ineffable deeds
    of a powerful mortal man.
He slew overweening Sinis
    who was supreme in strength,
the child of Earthshaker, son
    of Kronos, Lytaian Poseidon.
And he has slain the sow,
    murderer of men,
in the glens of Kremmyon
    and Skiron the arrogant,
and checked the wrestling place
    of Kerkyon, and the Chopper
has dropped the sturdy hammer
    of Polypemon: he met
a better man. I fear

the end of all this.
Who does he say is
    this man, and from where?
What armament has he?
    Does he bring a great host
with hostile weaponry?
    Or does he come alone
with his attendants like
    a merchant wandering to
a foreign land, so sturdy
    and strong and bold and who
has stayed the mighty strength
    of such a number of men?
Surely a god speeds him
    to devise their just due
for unjust men, for not
    easily does the ever-
active fail to fall
    upon evil. In the length of time
all will be accomplished.
    Two alone, he reports,
accompany him. He has
    about his shining shoulders
a sword of ivory haft
    and in his two hands
polished javelins,
    a Lakonian cap upon
his fiery auburn locks,
    a crimson cape about
his chest and a woolly cloak
    from Thessaly, and from
his eyes there flashes as from
    the volcano on Lemnos a flare
of flame red. He is
    in the first flush of youth,
intent on Ares' toys
    and the brazen battle clash,
and he comes in quest of Athens,
    the city that glories in splendor.

Paian IV

To the Pythian Apollo at Asine

Peace brings to birth for mortals
    confident wealth and blossoms
of honey-tongued songs,
    and upon the altars,
curiously wrought,
    there burn with umber flame
the thighs of oxen
    and fleecy sheep.
The youths delight in sport
    and flutes and festive dance.
In the iron-bound hasp
    are webs of rufous spiders,
and rust coats over
    the lance-headed spears,
the double-edged swords.
    There is no brazen trumpet's blare,
nor is there stripped from our lids
    the sleep of honeyed heart
that soothes the soul toward dawn.
    The streets brim
with lovely carousings,
    and the songs of children
flare like flame.

Paian VI

Don’t look for the tracks of a lurking bear .

PINDAR

Olympian I

For Hiero of Syracuse
Winner in the Horse Race, 476 B.C.

Turn 1
Water is best, but gold blazing like fire
in the night surpasses all lordly wealth.
If you wish, my heart,
to celebrate the games,
seek no star
shining by day more warm through
    the empty air than the sun,
nor a contest better to sing than Olympia,
whence the famous hymn embraces
the wits of the skilled to celebrate
Kronos' son, as they come to the rich
and blessed hearth of Hiero, *(1–11)*

Counter-turn 1
who wields his scepter of law in Sicily,
rich in flocks, culling the crests of every excellence,
glorified too
in blossom of song,
such joy do we often take
at his friendly board.
    But take from its peg the Dorian lyre
if any grace of Pisa and Pherenikos
puts thoughts most sweet in your mind
when beside the Alpheus he sped
without goad through the course
and laid his master in victory's arms, *(12–22)*

Stand 1
the Syracusan horse-delighting king. His fame shines
in Lydian Pelops' settlement of noble men.
Him the Earth-upholder of mighty strength
Poseidon loved, when from the bright cauldron Klotho
lifted him, his ivory shoulder all agleam.
Indeed, marvels are many, but tales

embroidered with intricate lies
seduce the wit of men beyond the truth. (23–29

Turn 2 Grace, who fashions for mortals every delight
and brings honor besides, often contrives to make
the unbelievable seem true.
Days to come will be
the wisest witnesses.
It is seemly for a man to speak
    good things about the gods. The blame is less.
Son of Tantalos, contradicting earlier men, I shall tell your tale.
When your father summoned the gods
to his elegant feast and to lovely Sipylos,
repaying their hospitality,
then the god of the gleaming trident snatched you up, (30–4

Counter-turn 2 his heart subdued to desire, and on his golden mares
he carried you to the highest house of wide-honored Zeus.
There, in another time,
Ganymede came
for the same need in Zeus.
When you had disappeared and no
    man's search returned you to your mother,
straightway some spiteful neighbor secretly said
that into the bubbling surface of boiling water
with a knife they sliced you limb by limb,
and at the tables about they divided and ate
every last bit of your flesh. (41–5

Stand 2 I cannot describe a god's gorging like this. I abhor.
Loss of gain is often the lot of slanderers.
If the scouts of Olympos honored any mortal,
that man was Tantalos. But he could not digest
his great prosperity. Satiety brought him
surpassing disaster, like the mighty stone
his father hung above him. Longing always
to cast it from his head, he wanders far from happiness. (52–

Turn 3 He has this helplessly shackled life,
a fourth labor with these, because he deceived the gods
and gave to his companions

nectar and ambrosia,
with which the gods had made
him immortal. If any man hopes
    to cheat a god, he is mistaken.
The immortals therefore sent the son back again
to the short-lived race of mortal men.
And when in his blossoming youth
his beard covered his chin black,
he bethought himself of a ready bride (59–69)

Counter-turn 3

from a Pisan father, glorious Hippodameia.
Approaching the foaming sea alone in the dark,
he called upon the deep-crashing
god of the goodly trident. To Pelops
he appeared close by, at his very foot.
To Poseidon Pelops said, "If the lovely gifts
    of Kypris, Poseidon, count at all
in my favor, impede Oinomaos' brazen spear
and upon the swiftest of chariots carry me
to Elis and to victory.
Thirteen suitors has he slain
and so delayed his daughter's (70–80)

Stand 3

marriage. Great danger does not overtake a strengthless man.
Of those who must die, who would sit in the dark
to keep at a simmer a nameless old age,
without a share of blessings? But upon this contest
I shall take my stand. Grant a lovely outcome."
So he spoke. Nor did he grasp at ineffectual
words. Glorifying him, the god
provided a golden car and unwearying horses with wings. (81–87)

Turn 4

He broke Oinomaos' strength to take the virgin bride,
who bore six sons eager in valorous deeds.
But now he lies among
the glorious dead
at the Alpheus' ford
in a tomb thronged by men
    beside an altar frequented by visitors. His fame
looks far from Olympia in the course
of Pelops, where swiftness of foot vies

and the peaks of strength, bold in toil.
The victor for the rest of his life
has honey-sweet fair skies, (88–9

Counter-turn 4

because of the games at least. The good that is day by day
comes best to every man. But I must crown
that one with equestrian strain
in Aiolic dance and song.
I am convinced that no host
more knowing of good,
more sovereign in power,
of living men, will I elaborate in famed folds of song.
A guardian god has mind, Hiero,
for your concerns. This is his care.
If he not abandon you too soon,
a still sweeter victory I hope (99–1

Stand 4

with swift chariot to celebrate, discovering a path
helpful for song as I come to conspicuous Kronion. For me
the Muse cherishes a shaft of surpassing strength.
Different men excel in different ways. The utmost crests
in kings. No longer peer afar.
May it be yours this time to tread on high,
and mine for all my days to mingle
with victors, foremost in every skill among the Hellenes. (110–

Olympian VI

For Hagesias of Syracuse
Winner in the Mule Chariot Race, 427(?) B.C.

Turn 1

As when, setting columns of gold
beneath the sturdy portico,
we build a marvelous megaron,
so the face of a work begun
must gleam from afar, and if one be
victor at Olympia,
steward of Zeus' mantic altar at Pisa,
fellow founder of glorious Syracuse,
what praise can he escape,
given ungrudging citizens,
in lovely strains of song? *(1–7)*

Counter-turn 1

Let the son of Sostratos know
that in this sandal he has
his heavenly foot. Valor without
danger is prized neither among men
nor in hollow ships. Many remember
if blessings come with toil.
Hagesias, prepared for you is the praise
Adrastos rolled in justice from his tongue
for the seer Oikleïdas, once,
Amphiaraos, when the earth snatched him
and his shining horses down. *(8–14)*

Stand 1

And then seven corpse fires burned
to the end and Talaos' son
spoke at Thebes some word like this:
"I long for my army's eye,
a skilled prophet and spear fighter
both." And this also
befits the Syracusan man, lord of the feast.
Neither disputatious nor overfond of victory,
I have sworn a mighty oath and clearly to him

I shall give witness of this, and the sweet-
voiced Muses will trust to me. (15–2

Turn 2

O Phintis, yoke for me now
the strength of mules,
and quickly, that on the bright path
I may mount the chariot and come
to the very seed of these men. For they,
leading the way, especially
know the road, for they received
garlands at Olympia. Now we must open
gates of song for them.
To Pitana and Eurotas' ford we must go
in season today. (22–2

Counter-turn 2

Pitana, they say, lay with Poseidon,
son of Kronos,
and bore Evadne, child of violet hair.
She hid in the folds of her robe her unwedded distress.
In the appointed month she summoned
her handmaids and bade
them carry to Eilatos' son the infant to rear.
At Phaisana he ruled Arkadian men and dwelt
beside the Alpheus by lot.
Reared there, she tasted first in Apollo's arms
the sweetness of Aphrodite. (29–

Stand 2

She did not escape Aipytos in all that time,
concealing the god's seed,
but to Pytho he went, pressing down in his heart
ineffable wrath with sharp concern,
to demand an oracle about
the unendurable disaster.
She, putting aside her sash, crimson dyed,
and silver pitcher, beneath the dark blue brake
was about to bear the prophetic boy. The golden-haired
god sent gentle Eleithyia to stand
beside her and the Fates too. (36–

Turn 3

There came from the lovely labor of her womb
Iamos straightway

to the light. In her anguish she laid him
upon the ground. Two green-eyed serpents
by the gods' intent nourished him
with blameless venom of bees, concernedly. The king,
riding back from rocky Pytho, asked
all in the house about
the child Evadne bore. For Phoibos, he said, had begotten him, *(43–49)*

Counter-turn 3
and he was destined to be a prophet beyond
all men on earth, nor would his race fail.
So he foretold. But they claimed not
to have heard nor seen the five-day-old
child, but he lay
hidden among the rushes in a deep thicket,
his delicate body drenched with the rays
of yellow and purple violets.
Wherefore his mother proclaimed that ever after *(50–56)*

Stand 3
he would be called by this name. And when
he plucked the fruit of gold-
garlanded Hebe, stepping down into Alpheus' stream,
he called upon Poseidon, wide in strength,
his forebear, and the bow-bedecked
guardian of god-built Delos,
begging for himself some fostering office,
beneath the night sky. There broke into ready speech
his father's voice, which said, "Rise, child,
and follow hither behind my voice
to a haunt common to all." *(57–63)*

Turn 4
They came to the sun-scorched rock of the son
of Kronos on high,
where he profferred to him a twofold treasure
of prophecy, then to hear the voice
that knew no lies, and when Herakles,
bold in battle, should come,
the Alkaïdai's sacred shoot, and for his father
found a festival, frequented of men,
and first ordinance of games,
then upon the top of the altar of Zeus
he bade him establish an oracle. *(64–70)*

Counter-turn 4

From him wide famed through Hellas
is the race of Iamidai.
Wealth followed after. Honoring valorous deeds,
they travel a visible road. Each thing
gives witness. Mockery from envious others
hovers above those
who drive first the twelve-lap course.
On them reverent Grace distills
glorious beauty of form.
If truly beneath the peak of Kyllene,
Hagesias, your mother's kin (71–7

Stand 4

dwell and present
the gods' herald with prayers and sacrifice,
frequently, with abundance and piety, Hermes,
who keeps the contests and fate of games,
and honors Arkadia, breeder of brave men,
he, O son of Sostratos,
with his deep-thundering father decrees your destiny.
I believe I have upon my tongue a shrill whetstone,
and there approaches me, willing, with rippling breeze,
my Stymphalian mother's mother,
beautifully blossoming Metope, (78–8

Turn 5

who bore Thebe, driver of horses,
whose water I drink,
weaving for men of the spear
an intricate song. Urge now your companions,
Aineas, to sing first of Hera,
goddess of maidenhood,
and then to know if in truth we escape
the ancient reproach, "Boiotian sow."
You are an honest messenger,
letter-staff of the Muses
of lovely hair, sweet mixing bowl of resounding songs. (85–

Counter-turn 5

I said to remember Syracuse
and Ortygia as well,
which Hiero with brilliant scepter disposes
with fitting concern, attending
Demeter of rosy feet and festival of

her daughter of white horses
and the power of Aitnaian Zeus. The sweet-
voiced lyres know him and the dance. May time
creeping on not shatter his wealth,
and with kindly courtesy may he receive
Hagesias' victory feast (92–98)

Stand 5

as it comes from house to house
from Stymphalian walls and leaves
his native Arkadia of lovely sheep.
Good in the stormy night
from the swift ship to sling
double anchors. May god
offer these friends and those glorious fate,
the sea's lord, and grant a voyage, straight
and free from distress, husband to Amphitrite
of golden spindle, and make grow
the blossoming joy of my song. (99–106)

Olympian VII

For Diagoras of Rhodes
Winner in the Boxing Match, 464 B.C.

Turn 1
As when one takes from an opulent hand a goblet
foaming within with the froth of the grape
and offers it
to the young bridegroom, betrothing from home to home, the
all-
golden peak of possessions,
and grace of the feast, honoring his
connection, and so among
friends makes him envied for his consenting bride, (1–6)

Counter-turn 1
so I, presenting the poured nectar, the Muses' gift,
to victorious men, the mind's sweet fruit,
make propitiation
to champions at Olympia and Pytho too. Blessed
whom good report embraces.
Grace, giving bloom of life, looks upon one man now,
another then, and with sweet lyre
often and with intricacy of full-voiced flutes. (7–12

Stand 1
Accompanied by both, with Diagoras I enter the lists to sing
the sea's child of Aphrodite
and Helios' bride, the island Rhodes,
to praise a huge straight-fisted man who won
garlands beside the Alpheus,
the booty of his boxing,
and beside Kastalia; his father too,
Damagetos, who pleases Right.
They dwell in the three-citied isle against
the thrust of spacious Asia, by right of Argive spear. (13–

Turn 2
I wish, beginning from Tlapolemos,
to bring news to straighten the common tale,
for Herakles' race,

broad in strength. For on their father's side they boast
descent from Zeus. The Amyntoridai,
on the mother's, from Astydameia. Errors
unnumbered hover
above the wits of men. Impossible to find (20–25)

Counter-turn 2

whatever now and in the end is best for a man.
For once the founder of this land,
striking with staff
of sturdy olive wood at Tiryns, in anger slew
as he came from Midea's chambers,
Likymnios, Alkmena's bastard brother.
Disturbances of wit
make even a wise man stray. He went for an oracle. (26–31)

Stand 2

To him the golden-haired god foretold from fragrant sanctuary
a voyage straight from the Lernaian cape
to the sea-washed stretch
where once the mighty king of gods drenched the city
with snowflakes of gold,
when by Hephaistos' device
with ax of beaten bronze Athena rose
from the crest of her father's head
and gave out the war cry, exceedingly loud.
Heaven shuddered at her and mother Earth. (32–38)

Turn 3

Then the son of Hyperion who brings light
to mortal men enjoined his children to keep
the coming injunction
that they be first to build for the goddess a brilliant altar
and make sacred sacrifice
to cheer the father's heart and that of the maid
of thundering spear. Respect
for forethought casts valor and grace upon men. (39–44)

Counter-turn 3

But a baffling cloud of forgetfulness descended upon
the men and drew the straight road of deeds
from out of their wits,
and they went up having not the seed of blazing flame.
They fashioned with fireless rites
a grove in the citadel. For them Zeus gathered

a yellow cloud and rained
abundant gold. The gray-eyed goddess provided them (45–50

Stand 3 with every skill of hand surpassing that of mortal men,
and their streets teemed with works
like live and creeping things.
Their renown went deep. For one who understands
skill is greater without deceit.
The ancient tales of men tell
that when Zeus and the other immortal gods
divided the earth, not yet
was Rhodes apparent upon the sea's main,
but the island lay hid in the salt depths. (51–5

Turn 4 In Helios' absence no one appointed him a share,
but they left him unallotted of land,
the holy god.
When he mentioned this, Zeus would have cast again, but he
forbade, since he said
that he himself had seen within the foaming sea,
blooming from its floor,
a land fostering mortals and mellow to flocks. (58–

Counter-turn 4 Straightway he bade Lachesis of golden diadem
to lift high her hands and not to forswear
the gods' mighty oath
but to nod with Kronos' child that, sent
to the shining air,
it would be his prize forevermore. The crests
of promises find accomplishment
falling in truth. There bloomed from the salt sea (64–

Stand 4 the island, which now the father of fierce rays has,
ruler of horses breathing flame,
where lying once with Rhodes he begat
seven sons displaying wisdom greater than that
of men in earlier times.
Of these one begat Kamiros,
and the eldest Ialysos. Lindos too
he begat. Separately they hold,
dividing in three their ancestral land,
their allotted towns, and they are called for them. (70–

Turn 5 There sweet requital for piteous disaster stands
for Tlapolemos, Tirynthian king,
as for a god,
smoking processionals of sheep and judgment of games.
With blossoms of these twice
was Diagoras crowned, and at famed Isthmos
four times fortunate;
at Nemea, win upon win, and at rocky Athens too. *(77–82)*

Counter-turn 5 In Argos the bronze knew him. In Arkadia
and Thebes, the toils, and the customary games
of Boiotians,
and Pellana. At Aigina he won six times.
In Megara no other tale
does the stony ballot tell. But, O Zeus father,
on Atabyrion's back
the sovereign, honor the Olympionician set of song *(83–88)*

Stand 5 and the hero whose excellence is boxing, and grant him grace
of respect from citizens and foreigners,
since he walks straight the path
hated by pride, knowing clearly what the wits
he has from his noble fathers
demand. Do not conceal the seed
common from Kallianax. With blessings
of Eratidai the city
also has festivities. In one portion of time
the breezes flare, now some here, now some there. *(89–95)*

Olympian XIII

For Xenophon of Corinth
Winner in the Footrace and Pentathlon, 464 B.C.

Turn 1

Thrice victors at Olympia
whose house I praise, gentle to citizens,
attentive to strangers, I shall know
wealthy Corinth, forecourt
of Isthmian Poseidon, city of shining youths.
There Order dwells and her sisters,
cities' secure foundation,
Justice and her sibling Peace, stewardess of wealth
to men, golden daughters of prudent Themis. *(1–8)*

Counter-turn 1

They will to ward off
Violence, bold-mouthed mother of Surfeit.
I have lovely things to say, and straight
daring urges my tongue to speak.
Impossible to hide native character.
For you, children of Alatas, often the Hours
have offered shining victory
as you ascended the peaks of excellence in sacred games
and into the hearts of men they often cast *(9–1*

Stand 1

in their abundant flowering
inventions of old. The founder's is every deed.
Where else did the graces of Dionysos
first appear with ox-driven dithyramb?
Who put curbs to the horses' gear
or the double king of birds upon the gods'
shrines? There the sweetly breathing Muse
blossoms, and Ares too
in the fierce spears of young men. *(17–*

Turn 2

Highest and ruling wide
over Olympia, ungrudging of words
may you be for all time, father Zeus,

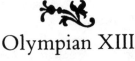

and keeping his people unharmed,
steer straight the wind of Xenophon's fate.
Accept for him this festive set of garlands
he brings from the plains of Pisa,
victorious in the stade and pentathlon too. No other
mortal before has achieved so much. (24–31)

Counter-turn 2

Two wreaths of parsley
crowned him when he appeared
at the Isthmos. Nemea, not otherwise.
For Thessalos, his father, beside the streams
of Alpheus, the glory of his feet is laid up.
At Pytho he won at the stade and the two-lap race
within a single sun, and in the same month,
at rocky Athens, one swift-footed day laid
three most beautiful wreaths upon his locks. (32–39)

Stand 2

At the Hellotian, seven times, and in
Poseidon's sea-girt precinct
with Ptoiodoros, their father, longer songs attend
Terpsias and Eritimos as well.
For all that you achieved at Delphi
or in the lion's pasturage, I contend with many
about the plentitude of blessings, but even I
could not accurately count
the pebbles in the sea. (40–46)

Turn 3

In each thing measure
is meet. Season is best to know.
Setting sail myself on a voyage common to all,
proclaiming ancestral wit
and heroic achievement in war,
I shall not lie about Corinth: Sisyphos,
most skilled in craft of hand, like a god,
and Medea, who married in her father's despite,
savior to Argo and all its crew. (47–54)

Counter-turn 3

Then too in strength
before Dardanos' walls they thought
on both sides to cut an end of battle,
these with Atreus' own seed

retrieving Helen, those altogether
preventing it. At Glaukos, coming
from Lykia, the Danaans trembled. To them
he boasted that in Peirene's town had been
his father's rule and deep domain and megaron. (55–62

Stand 3 That Bellerophon
suffered much when once he longed beside
the springs to yoke the snake-haired Gorgon's son,
Pegasos, until there offered him the bridle,
gold bedecked, the virgin Pallas. From his dream straightway
a waking vision, she said, "Do you sleep, Aiolian king?
Accept this equestrian charm and to
the Tamer Poseidon offer it
with sacrifice of shining bull." (63–69

Turn 4 As he slumbered in the dark,
the maid of blue-black aegis seemed
to speak to him. He leapt straight up.
Gathering the portent beside him,
in joy he sought the indigenous seer,
and showed to Koiranos' son all the end
of the affair, how he had slept beside the altar
of the goddess by night at his behest
and how the child of Zeus
of the thundering spear had offered him (70–7

Counter-turn 4 the spirit-subduing gold.
He bade him obey the dream immediately,
and when he had drawn back the bull's head
for the Earth-upholder, wide in strength,
to found an altar straightway to Athena of Horses.
The power of gods makes light the possession
of things beyond oath or expectation.
Mighty Bellerophon,
pondering, caught,
stretching the gentle charm to the jaw, (78–

Stand 4 the winged steed. Mounting, straightway,
he made play in panoply of bronze,
with arms, and on that horse once,

from the chill gulfs of empty air
he smote and slew the archer host of Amazons,
the Chimaira, snorting fire, and the Solymoi.
Of his fate I shall keep silent,
but Pegasos the ancient mangers
of Zeus received on Olympos. *(86–92)*

Turn 5
I must not cast a whirl
of darts beyond the mark and so
empower numerous shafts with my hands.
To the Muses on shining thrones I came,
willingly, with aid, and to the Oligaïthidai.
Their thronging deeds at the Isthmos and Nemea
I shall make manifest in few words, but a true
and sworn witness, sixty times at each place,
for me will be the noble herald's sweet-tongued shout. *(93–100)*

Counter-turn 5
What they did at Olympia
it befitted me before to say.
Achievements to come I shall make clear
at the time. Now I have hope; in god
is the end. But if their native divinity proceed,
to Zeus and Enyalios we shall entrust
accomplishment of this. Beneath Parnassos' brow,
six times. At Argos as often and in Thebes.
Of the same in Arkadian glens
Lykaios' lordly altar will give witness. *(101–8)*

Stand 5
Pellana and Sikyon,
Megara and the fenced grove of Aiakidai,
Eleusis and shining Marathon,
the beautifully rich cities of high-crested Aitna
and Euboia: all through Hellas
you will find, if you seek, more than one can see.
Now with nimble feet let me swim.
Zeus accomplisher, grant reverence
and sweet chance of delight. *(109–15)*

Pythian I

For Hiero of Aitna
Winner in the Chariot Race, 470 B.C.

Turn 1

Golden lyre, of Apollo and the violet-plaited
Muses the common possession, which the dance step
hears and begins the radiance,
the singers obey your notes
whenever, struck aquiver, you fashion
the preludes' enticing choruses
and quench even the spearing thunderbolt
of ever-flowing fire. There sleeps atop
the scepter of Zeus the eagle, folding
from either side his swift pinion, *(1–6)*

Counter-turn 1

king of birds; you shed a dark mist upon
his hooked head, sweet closure
of eyelids. Slumbering,
he ripples his lissome back, enchanted
by your rippling drafts. Even
violent Ares, abandoning the edge
of harsh swords, allows his heart to melt
in deep sleep. Your shafts of song beguile
even the deities' wits, by the skill
of Leto's son and the full-breasted Muses. *(7–12*

Stand 1

All that Zeus loves not are distraught
at the Pierides' cry throughout the land
and on the irresistible sea,
and he who lies in dire Tartaros, the gods' foe,
Typho of the hundred heads, whom once
the Kilikian cave of many names nourished, but now
Kyme's seagirt banks
and Sicily suppress
his shaggy chest, and heaven's column,
snowy Aitna, crushes him too,
yearlong nurse of piercing frosts, *(13–2*

Turn 2

from which erupt most holy fountains of
unapproachable fire from his depths. By day
rivers pour forth a flaming stream
of smoke. But in the dark, a scarlet blaze
rolls rocks to the deep flat of the sea,
crashing resoundingly.
That monster spews forth Hephaistos'
most awesome springs: a portent
marvelous to see and a wonder
for men nearby to hear, *(21–26)*

Counter-turn 2

such is he, bound beneath Aitna's black-leaved peaks
and the plain, and his jagged couch cards all
his back cramped against it.
May it be ours, O Zeus, to please you
who haunt this mountain, the brow
of the fruited land whose famous founder
has glorified its namesake city
neighboring near. In the Pythian course
the herald proclaimed her,
announcing Hiero's lovely victory *(27–32)*

Stand 2

with chariots. For seafaring men first grace
for setting sail is the coming on of escorting
wind. For probable then
in the end is achievement of better return, and thought
on these occurrences brings expectation
of a city forever famed for horses and wreaths,
renowned for euphonious celebrations.
Lykian and lord of Delos,
Phoibos, who love Parnassos and Kastalian spring,
may you will all this with your mind
and make the land blessed in its men. *(33–40)*

Turn 3

From the gods is every device for mortal excellence,
and men are skilled and strong of hand
and eloquent. That man I expect
passionately to praise
so as not to cast the brazen-cheeked javelin
whirling it outside the lists,
but hurling it far to outstrip my antagonists.

May all time steer him toward prosperity
and the gift of possessions
and offer forgetfulness of ills. (41–4

Counter-turn 3

Indeed, he might recall in what battles of war
with enduring heart he stood steadfast, when
men found at the gods' hands honor
such as no one else of the Hellenes plucks,
a lordly garland of wealth. But now in truth,
taking Philoktetes' way,
he made campaign. Under constraint
even a proud man fawns for his friendship.
They say that from Lemnos
the godlike heroes came to board (47–5

Stand 3

the archer, Poias' son, worn with his wound.
He sacked Priam's citadel and put an end
to the Danaans' tribulations.
He stepped with infirm flesh, but he was doom.
Thus may god bring Hiero restoration,
granting for creeping time, in season, his heart's desire.
Muse, I bid you beside Deinomenes to sing
recompense for the four-horsed chariot race.
Not foreign to him the joy of his father's victory.
Now next for the king of Aitna
let us discover a song to be his own. (53–

Turn 4

For him Hiero founded that city, with freedom
god-built, and in the laws of Hyllos' decrees.
The descendants of Pamphylos wish,
and indeed the Herakleidai as well,
dwelling beneath Taÿgetos' peaks,
to abide in Aigimios' ordinance,
Dorians. Blessed, they acquired Amyklai,
setting forth from Pindos, neighbors, in glory profound,
to the Tyndaridai of white colts,
and their spears blossomed to fame. (61–

Counter-turn 4

Zeus accomplisher, forever beside Amenas' waters
may the true account of men assign such fate
to citizens and kings alike.

With your help may this leader, this hero,
enjoining his son, honoring his folk,
turn them to harmonious peace.
Nod, I beg you, son of Kronos, that throughout
a quiet house the Phoinikian and Etruscan
battle cry be checked, seeing the ship-
wrecked violence off the coast at Kyme (67–72)

Stand 4
and what they suffered, overcome by the Syracusan lord,
who from their swift-faring ships hurled
their youth into the sea,
dragging Hellas free from slavery's weight. I pray
from Salamis, for the Athenians' grace
as my wage; in Sparta, from the battle before Kithairon,
in which the Medes of the bent bow faltered,
and beside the well-watered strand
of Himera by completing a song for Deinomenes' sons,
which they deserved for their valor
when their enemy went down. (73–80)

Turn 5
If you should speak in season, drawing taut the strands
of much in brief, less blame would follow from men,
for dismal satiety blunts
the edge of swift hopes.
What citizens hear weighs secretly upon the soul,
especially if it concerns the blessings of others.
Nevertheless, for envy is better than pity,
do not forgo the fair. Steer with just
rudder the host. Forge your tongue
upon an anvil innocent of lies. (81–86)

Counterturn 5
If anything paltry sparks, it is called great
coming from you. You are steward of much. Many
are the witnesses, and credible, to both.
Abiding in blossoming disposition,
if you would hear, always, sweet report,
do not falter overmuch in bounty.
Like a ship's pilot let go your sail
full to the wind. Be not beguiled,
O friend, by a profit easily
turned. The vaunt of glory to come (87–92)

Stand 5 alone declares when men are gone their way of life
to bards and tellers of tales. Kroisos' generosity
    does not diminish,
but infamy everywhere oppresses Phalaris
of pitiless intent, who roasted men in the bronze bull.
No lyres beneath the roof welcome him as theme
to be sweetly shared in the songs of boys.
To fare well is the first of rewards.
Good repute is the next best fate. The man
who chances upon and takes the two
receives the highest crown of all. *(93–10*

Pythian II

For Hiero of Syracuse
Winner in the Chariot Race at the Theban Iolaia, 476(?) B.C.

Turn 1
Magnificent city, Syracuse, precinct of Ares
plungeed in war, of heroes and horses delighting
in weaponry the divine nurse,
I come bringing to you from shining Thebes
a song to proclaim the four-horse race that shakes the earth
in which Hiero, nobly charioted, won
and bound with wreaths that gleam from afar Ortygia,
the haunt of the rivers' Artemis; not without her
did he with gentle hands master those colts
with their embroidered reins. *(1–8)*

Counter-turn 1
The virgin archeress with two hands
and Hermes of the games lay on the glittering tack
whenever he yokes to his polished car
and wheels obedient to the bit
his horses' strength, and calls upon the god of the trident, wide in force.
Different bards for different kings compose
melodious song as recompense for excellence.
There echo often the songs of Kyprians
for Kinyras whom golden-haired Apollo
loved, cherishingly, *(9–16)*

Stand 1
docile priest of Aphrodite. The grace of friends
comes to gaze in reverence for deeds done.
But you, O son of Deinomenes, before the house
the Lokrian maid of the West Wind proclaims.
After hopeless hardships of war
because of your power her grace is steadfast.
At the gods' behest Ixion, they say, to mortals told this
as he on his winged wheel
was spun round and round:

Requite your benefactor
with kindly recompense. (17–24)

Turn 2 He learned too well. For though among the gracious children of
Kronos
he had got a sweet life, he tolerated not extensive
prosperity, when with maddened wits
he lusted after Hera, who belonged to Zeus'
bed of delight. Infatuation drove him
to conspicuous folly, and soon, suffering what fits a man,
he met with choice distress. Both his sins
blossomed with toil, for that hero was first,
not without guile, to imbue the mortal race
with the blood of kin, (25–32

Counter-turn 2 and then in the large, concealing bridal room
he touched the wife of Zeus. One must look to oneself
for the measure of everything.
Aberrant embraces have cast men down to evils
profound. They overtook him as well, because
he lay in love with a cloud,
pursuing a sweet deceit, the ignorant man,
a phantom resembling the Ouranians' eminence,
the daughter of Kronos. The hands of Zeus had set
the snare before him, a lovely bane. The four-spoked
bond he fashioned himself, (33–4

Stand 2 his own doom. Entangled in inescapable bonds,
he received the message common to all.
Without the Graces she bore him a monstrous child,
unique the mother, unique the son, unhonored
among men and in the ordinances of gods.
She reared and named him Kentauros, and he
mingled with Magnesian mares on the spurs
of Pelion, and there was begotten a host
marvelous to look upon, to both
parents like; from the mother
below, from the father above. (41–4

Turn 3 God achieves each end as he expects,
god, who overtakes the winged eagle and
surpasses the dolphin

of the sea and bends to his will the haughty man;
to others he offers glory that ages not. I must
eschew the excessive bite of calumny.
Though distant, I have often seen censorious
Archilochos fattening helplessly
on slanderous enmity. Wealth with wisdom
is best of destiny. (49–56)

Counter-turn 3 Clearly you can show this with freedom of heart,
prince and lord of many battlemented streets
and the host, and if anyone
claims that another of men before in Hellas
surpassed you in either possessions or honor,
with gaping wit he wrestles emptiness.
I shall mount the beautifully blossoming prow to sing
of excellence. Boldness aids youth
in dreadful wars, and so I say that you
have found boundless fame (57–64)

Stand 3 for fighting among warriors on horseback
and foot soldiers too. Your mature counsels
allow me word of praise without risk for the full
account. And so farewell!
Like Phoinikian merchandise
this song is sped across the foaming sea.
Willingly behold the Kastorian song on Aiolian strings,
welcoming it by grace
of the seven-toned lyre.
Be what you know you are.
A pretty thing to children is the ape, always (65–72)

Turn 4 pretty. But Rhadamanthys fared well, because
he had as his lot that blameless fruit of mind, nor
does he delight his heart with deceits
such as always haunt a man at the hands of whisperers.
Resistless evil to both are the stealthy words of slanderers,
exactly like foxes in disposition.
But what does the fox gain by this?
While the rest of the tackle toils
in the salt depths, I undrenched, like a cork,
float above the brine. (73–80)

Counter-turn 4

A deceitful citizen cannot cast a word of force
among noble men. Nevertheless he fawns on all
    and weaves everywhere a web of ruin.
I do not share his daring. May I befriend my friend.
Against my foe, like a wolf
    I shall turn to attack,
treading, now here, now there, on devious tracks.
In every government the straight-tongued man comes
to the fore, in tyranny or when the boisterous host
or when the wise keep the city in guard. One must
    not contend with a god (81–88

Stand 4

who now exalts the power of these, and now to those
    awards enormous glory. Not even this soothes
the mind of envious men. Stretching the measuring line
excessively, they puncture
    with piercing wound their own hearts
before achieving what they contrive in anxiety.
To bear lightly the yoke one takes upon one's neck
is best. To kick against
the goad, you know,
is a slippery path. May I
    please and consort with noble men. (89–9

Pythian III

For Hiero of Syracuse
Victor in the Horse Race, 482, 478 B.C.

Turn 1 Would that Chiron, son of Philyra—
if I must from my own tongue
tell the common prayer—
dead and gone were alive today,
the son, broad in sway, of Ouranian Kronos,
and reigned, that rugged beast, in Pelian glens,
his mind kindly to men. Such was he when once he reared
gentle Asklepios, architect
of limb-relieving anodynes,
that hero who helped in maladies of every kind. *(1–7)*

Counter-turn 1 Before the daughter of Phlegyas of beautiful steeds
could bring him to birth with Eleithyia attendant,
destroyed by Artemis' arrows of gold
in her marriage chamber, she descended to Hades' house
by Apollo's device. Not vain the anger
of the children of Zeus. But she flouted it
in a wandering of wits
and agreed to another marriage in secret from her father,
although she had lain before with Apollo of the unshorn hair *(8–14)*

Stand 1 and carried the god's seed;
nor did she await the bridal feast
or the full ringing tones of the wedding hymns
that girl companions of her own age love
in the evenings playfully to sing. No,
she fell in love with what was afar. As many have done.
There is among men a most foolish tribe,
disgracing what is native and gazing afar
to chase with futile hopes what is borne on the winds. *(15–23)*

Turn 2 Such infatuation captured the will
of the lovely-robed Koronis, for she slept
in the bed of a stranger

who came from Arkadia, but she
did not escape the watcher. For though he was
at sheep-receiving Pytho, the lord of the shrine,
Loxias, knew, persuaded by an unerring informer,
in his omniscient mind.
He does not fasten on lies, and there deceives him
neither mortal nor god in deed or plan. (24–3(

Counter-turn 2 So then he knew of her coupling with a foreigner,
Ischys, Eilatos' son, and of her lawless deceit,
and sent his sister, raging
with irresistible might,
to Lakereia, since the unwed girl dwelt
beside the banks of Boibias. Her genius
turned to evil and mastered her, and many
neighbors shared her fate and perished
with her. On a mountain, fire
that leaps from a single seed destroys a great wood. (31–3

Stand 2 But when her kin had placed the girl
inside her coffin's wooden walls, and Hephaistos'
voracious flame ran round about, then Apollo said,
"No longer can I in my heart endure to destroy
my own child with its mother's most piteous death
and grievous suffering." So he spoke and with single stride
snatched
the child from the corpse. The fire blazed apart for him.
He carried the babe to Magnesian Kentauros to learn
the healing of the painful illnesses of men. (38–

Turn 3 As many as came with flesh-grown sores
or with limbs wounded by the gray bronze
or boulder thrown from afar
or with bodies ravaged by fiery heat
or cold, he freed from their various pains
and delivered them, attending some with soothing incantations
and others with potions,
or by wrapping their limbs around
with simples, and some he restored with the knife. (47–

Counter-turn 3 But even skill is enthralled by gain.
Gold apparent upon the palm reduced even him

with princely wage
to bring back from the dead a man
already taken. With his hands, therefore, Kronos' son,
ripping their breath from both their chests,
slew them swiftly; his blazing thunderbolt inflicted death.
One must seek from the gods
what is possible for mortal minds
and know what is at hand and what our destiny. *(54–60)*

Stand 3 Do not, my soul, be eager for
immortal life; exhaust the practicable device.
If only wise Chiron were living yet in his cave,
and if my honey-sweet songs cast some spell
on his soul, I surely should have persuaded him
to send to noble men a healer of burning fevers,
someone called the son of Leto or of his father Apollo.
And on ships I should have come, cleaving the Ionian Sea
to Arethousa's spring and to my Aitnaian host *(61–69)*

Turn 4 who rules Syracuse, a king,
gentle to citizens, unenvying of nobles,
to foreigners a wondrous father.
And if with double grace
I had disembarked, bringing golden health
and the song's gleam for wreaths from Pythian games
which once Pherenikos won, excelling at Kirrha,
like the far-shining light
of a heavenly star, I say, I should
have come to him, crossing the deep sea. *(70–76)*

Counter-turn 4 But I wish myself to offer prayer
to the Mother whom the maidens before my door,
together with Pan, often hymn
at night, the goddess revered.
But if you have the wit, O Hiero, to understand
the correct crown of words of earlier men,
you know the immortals apportion to men two sorrows
for every good. These foolish mortals
cannot bear becomingly,
but noble men can, turning the fair without. *(77–83)*

Stand 4 But you the lot of blessedness attends,

for magnificent destiny casts her glance upon
his people's leader, the tyrant, if upon any man. A life secure
did not belong to Peleus, Aiakos' son,
nor to godlike Kadmos, who, they say, attained
of mortal men the highest happiness, for they heard
the Muses, golden diademed, upon the mountain
and at seven-gated Thebes singing when one married ox-eyed
Harmonia, the other Thetis, famed daughter of prudent Nereus. (84–92

Turn 5 And the gods banqueted with both of them,
and they saw the royal sons of Kronos
    on golden thrones, and received
wedding gifts. By grace of Zeus
released from earlier troubles, they were
    of cheerful heart. In turn, in time,
his three daughters by their keen sufferings
made Kadmos bereft of his share
of happiness. But
    Zeus the father came to the lovely bed
of Thyone of the ivory arms. (93–9

Counter-turn 5 Peleus' son, the only one that immortal
Thetis bore in Phthia, abandoned his soul
    to arrows in war
and roused as he burned on the pyre
the Danaans' lamentation. But if any mortal keeps
    the path of truth in mind, he must
by immortal grace fare well. Now here, now there
flare the high-flown winds.
    Not for long does men's prosperity come
secure, when it attends with weight and quantity. (100–

Stand 5 Small among small estate, great among great
shall I be. My attendant genius of mind
I shall forever cultivate and cherish my skill.
But if a god should extend to me luxurious wealth,
I hope to find in future days lofty fame.
Nestor and Lykian Sarpedon of men's report we know
from ringing lays that architects of skill
fashioned for them. Excellence by illustrious song
is feted long, but accomplishment is easy for few. (107–

Pythian IV

For Arkesilas of Kyrene
Winner in the Chariot Race, 462 B.C.

Turn 1

Today you must stand beside a dear man,
the king of Kyrene of beautiful horses,
    so that with Arkesilas triumphant,
my Muse, and that for the children of Leto and Pytho too,
    you may increase the wind of song owed to them,
where once, seated beside the golden eagles of Zeus,
Apollo not far away, the priestess
prophesied that Battos would colonize
    fruitful Libya that he might leave
the holy island at once and found a city
of beautiful chariots on the gleaming breast of the sea, *(1–8)*

Counterturn 1

and bring to pass Medea's word,
in the seventeenth generation, spoken
    at Thera, which once Aietes' inspired
daughter breathed from her immortal lips,
the Kolchian princess. She spoke thus
to the demigod sailors of spearman Jason:
"Listen, sons of high-spirited mortals and gods.
I say that from this sea-washed land
    in time the daughter of Epaphos
will plant in herself the root cherished by men,
in the precincts of Zeus Ammon. *(9–16)*

Stand 1

"Exchanging short-finned dolphins
    for swift steeds,
and oars for reins, they drive chariots
    with wheels like the winds.
That portent shall bring it to pass that Thera
become the mother of mighty cities, the token that
    in the outfall of Tritonian lake once
Euphamos, as he stepped down from the prow, took
from a god in guise of a man who offered him earth

as a guest-gift—propitiously the son of Kronos,
father Zeus, crashed his thunder— (17–23)

Turn 2
"when he chanced upon us as we slung upon
the ship the brazen-cheeked anchor, swift
Argo's bit. For twelve days before
we had carried from Ocean over
desolate ridges of land
the sea's bark, drawing it up by my advice.
Then the lonely divinity approached; he
wore the shining countenance of
a revered man, and began
with the friendly words of beneficent hosts
who first invite strangers to dine. (24–31

Counter-turn 2
"But reason of sweet return to home
prevented our lingering. He declared that he
was Eurypylos, the immortal Earthshaker's
son. He recognized that we were pressing on and snatched
straightway a piece of earth
and sought to give as a guest-gift what came to hand,
nor did Euphamos disobey, but the hero leapt upon the strand
and, pressing hand to hand,
accepted the divine clod.
But I understand that it was washed far from the ship
into the sea and went with the salt spray (32–3

Stand 2
"at eventide to follow the watery main. Indeed,
again and again I urged
the deckhands on watch to guard
it well. But their wits forgot,
and now the imperishable seed of broad Libya
is washed to this island before its time. For if
at home he had cast it beside
Hades' chthonic mouth, coming to holy Tainaron,
Euphamos, son of Poseidon, lord of horses,
whom once Europa, Tityos' daughter,
bore beside Kephisos' banks, (40–4

Turn 3
"the blood of the fourth generation from him
would with the Danaoi have taken
that broad continent. For then men

rise and go from mighty Lakedaimon
    and gulf of Argos and from Mykenai.
But now he will find in foreign women's beds
    a choice generation that with the grace of gods
will come to this island and here beget
    a mortal to be the lord of the dark-
clouded plains, whom in his gold-bedecked house
Phoibos will mention in oracles,
as he descends to the Pythian shrine in later
time, as bringing many men in ships
    to the fertile precinct of the Nile's Zeus." *(47–54)*

Counter-turn 3 Thus Medea's verses, and the godlike heroes
    cowered and stood, in silence,
quite still, hearing her prescient counsel.
O blessed son of Polymnastos, you it was
that the oracle exalted in this prophecy
    by inspired song of the Delphic bee.
She hailed you thrice, ringingly, and revealed you
as destined king of Kyrene, *(55–62)*

Stand 3 when you asked what recompense you would have
    from the gods for your stuttering.
Indeed, even now in aftertime, as at
    the prime of rosy-budding spring,
eighth in line from those sons Arkesilas blooms.
To him Apollo and Pytho offered glory from
the dwellers-about for victory
in the chariot race. To the Muses I shall present him
and the all-golden fleece of the ram. For after that,
when the Minyans sailed, god-sent honors
    were planted for them. *(63–69)*

Turn 4 How did they begin their voyaging?
What peril bound them with sturdy nails
    of adamant? An oracle had said that Pelias
would die at the hands of noble Argonauts
    or by inflexible plots.
There had come to him a prophecy to chill his soul,
beside the navel stone of the forested mother
to keep complete and serious guard

against the single-sandaled man
whenever from the steep steadings he should come
to the land seen from afar of famed Iolkos, (70–7

Counter-turn 4
whether citizen or foreigner. And so in time
he came, with twin spears, a terrifying
man. In two fashions clothed,
his native Magnesian dress fitted close
his marvelous limbs,
and a leopard skin kept off the shivery rains.
Nor did his glorious locks go shorn
but blazed all down his back.
Straightway he strode and stood
to try his unaffrighted soul at the hour
when throngs were crowding the marketplace. (78–8

Stand 4
They knew him not. Nevertheless, one of those
who gazed spoke and said this:
"I don't suppose that this is Apollo
nor Aphrodite's spouse of brazen
chariot. On gleaming Naxos, they say, the sons
of Iphimedeia died, Otos and you,
Epialtas, daring king.
And surely the swift shaft of Artemis hunted
Tityos down, sped from her unconquerable quiver,
that a man might lust to touch only those loves
within his power." (86–

Turn 5
So they muttered to one another and said
things like this. But with mules
and polished cart Pelias came,
speeding headlong. He was at once amazed
as he spied the sandal, conspicuous
upon the right foot alone. But he hid his fear
in his heart and said, "What land, O stranger,
do you claim is yours? And which of earthborn
mortals spewed you forth
from her withered womb? Tell and do not stain
with most disgusting lies your race." (93–

Counter-turn 5
Courageously, with gentle words, the stranger
made reply, "I declare that I shall bear

the teaching of Chiron, for from his cave I come,
from Chariklo and Philyra, where Kentauros'
holy daughters reared me.
In all my twenty years with neither deed
nor spoken word to cause them shame I come
home to recover the ancient honor
of my father, wielded now
not with right, which once Zeus bestowed upon
Aiolos, the people's chief, and his sons. *(101–8)*

Stand 5 "For I hear that Pelias, lawlessly, persuaded by
his jealous passion,
reft it forcefully from my parents of primal right.
But they, when first I saw the light, in fear
of the overweening leader's violence, as though
for one dead, made somber
lamentation within the house where the women keened,
and in crimson swaddling clothes they sent me in secret,
making the night the journey's confidant, to Chiron,
Kronos' son, to rear. *(109–15)*

Turn 6 "But you know my story's summary. Now,
cherished citizens, show me clearly the house
of my fathers who rode white horses,
for I am Aison's son, a native, nor do I come
to a foreign land of other men.
The divine beast was wont to call me Jason."
So he spoke. As he entered, his father's eyes
recognized him, and tears bubbled up
from his ancient lids,
for he rejoiced in his soul when he saw
his choice son, most handsome of men. *(116–23)*

ounter-turn 6 And both his father's brothers came
upon the report. From close by,
Pheres, leaving the Hyperian spring,
and from Messana, Amythan. And swiftly
Admetos came and Melampos,
in kindness toward their cousin. In sharing the feast,
Jason received them with gentle words;
providing fitting hospitality,

he extended all festivity,
plucking for five full nights and days
the sacred blossom of bliss. (124–

Stand 6 But on the sixth the hero told all his tale
from beginning to end earnestly,
sharing it with his kin.
They followed him. At once from their seats
he leapt with them, and they came to Pelias' megaron.
Rushing within, they took their stand. And he,
when he heard, stepped forth to greet them,
the son of Tyro of lovely locks. Jason, distilling
with soft voice a gentle speech,
laid the foundation stone of wise words:
"Son of Poseidon, Cleaver of Rocks, (132–

Turn 7 "mortal wits are rather quick to praise
deceitful gain above righteousness although
they crawl to the harsh reckoning day.
But you and I must control our dispositions
to weave prosperity for time to come.
I shall tell you what you know. One heifer was mother
to Kretheus and Salmoneus, bold in counsel. In the third
generation, sprung from them,
we look upon the golden strength
of the sun. The Fates withdraw, if any enmity
divides kin, to hide their shame. (139

Counter-turn 7 "It befits us not with brazen-forged swords
or javelins to divide the mighty sovereignty
of our fathers. I concede to you
the flocks and tawny herds of cattle and all
the fields you stole away
from our parents and work to fatten your wealth.
It pains me not that they provide your house
excessively. But the royal scepter
and throne where once the son of Kretheus
sat, dispensing righteous judgment to his horsemen people—
these without common vexation to us (14

Stand 7 "release, lest some fresh trouble for us
arise from them."

So then he spoke, and Pelias in turn
made gentle reply, "I will be such.
But now the lot of ancient age
attends me. For you the bloom of youth
just swells. You have the strength to remove
the wrath of chthonic gods. For Phrixos bids us
recover his soul, going to Aietes' halls,
and bring the deep-fleeced hide of the ram
by which once he was saved from the deep (155–61)

Turn 8 "and from his stepmother's godless shafts.
This a wondrous dream came and told
to me. At Kastalia I asked the oracle
if anything need be sought. It bade me fashion
as soon as I could an escort of ship.
This task be willing to complete, and monarchy
and kingdom I swear to release to you.
As a powerful pledge let our common ancestral
Zeus be witness to this."
This covenant they approved and parted.
But Jason himself straightway (162–69)

Counter-turn 8 sent heralds everywhere to declare
that the voyage would be. Immediately
three sons of Kronian Zeus, unwearying
in battle came, one from glancing-eyed Alkmena
and two from Leda; and two heroes
with high-waving hair, Poseidon's progeny, respecting strength,
from Pylos and Tainaron's' cape. For them and Euphamos
noble glory found fulfillment
and for you, Periklymenos, wide in strength.
From Apollo there came the harper, father of songs,
Orpheus the famed. (170–77)

Stand 8 Hermes of golden wand sent twin sons
to the unabating toil,
both exulting in youth, Echion
and Erytos. And quickly came
those who dwell at the foot of Pangaion,
for willingly had Boreas, the king of the winds,
with rejoicing heart

equipped Zetes and Kalais, heroes whose backs
rippled at either side with crimson wings,
and all-persuasive sweet desire did Hera
enkindle in the demigods (178–8

Turn 9

for the ship Argo, lest anyone left behind
remain at his mother's side to coddle
a life without risk, but rather, even
with meed of death discover with other companions
that lovely elixir of valor.
When there came down to lolkos the flower
of seamen, Jason counted and praised them all. For him
Mopsos, the seer, prophesying
by birds and sacred lots,
willingly put the host on board. When they had slung
the anchor upon the prow, (185–

Counter-turn 9

taking in his hands a golden goblet,
the leader, standing at the stern, called upon Zeus
of thundering spear, father of heaven's sons,
and the swift blasts of wind and wave
and nights and paths of the deep
and for propitious days and friendly fate of voyage home.
From the clouds there sounded in reply thunder's
portentous voice, and there burst forth
the flashing spokes of the lightning bolt.
The heroes drew breath, putting their trust
in the god's signs. The seer signaled (193–

Stand 9

to them to bend to their oars, inspiring them
with sweet hopes.
The rowing made water give way from the speed
of their hands, insatiate.
Sped by a southwest wind, they came to the mouth
of the Euxine and established there a sacred precinct
of Poseidon, god of the sea,
and ruddy flocks of Thracian bulls were there
and the newly built hollowed top of an altar of stones.
Speeding to danger profound,
they invoked the lord of ships (201-

Turn 10

that they might escape the irresistible clash
of colliding rocks, for they were twin and alive,
and they rolled more quickly than
the ranks of the deep-thudding winds. But
  that voyage of demigods now
brought them death. And then to Phasis
they went, where with the swarthy Kolchians
they mingled force in the realm of Aietes himself.
  The lady of swift darts, from Olympos,
yoked the dappled wryneck to the four-spoked
  ceaseless wheel, (208–15)

Counter-turn 10

and she, the Kypros-born, brought the maddening bird
for the first time to men and taught Aison's son
  supplications and charms,
that he might make Medea bereft of reverence
  for parents and longing for Hellas
with persuasion's whip lash her with mind ablaze.
Soon she revealed how to achieve her father's tasks.
Mixing with oil cut herbs
  as antidote for stark pain,
she gave anointment to him, and they agreed
  to sweet marriage between them. (216–23)

Stand 10

But when Aietes had planted in their midst
  the adamantine plow
and the bulls that breathed from tawny jaws
  flame of blazing fire
were with brazen hooves smiting the ground,
alone he led and yoked them to the plow.
  Stretching the furrows straight,
he drove and split the back of the clodded earth
a fathom deep, and spoke thus: "Let the king
who commands the ship, completing this task for me,
  take the indestructible coverlet, (224–30)

Turn 11

"the gleaming fleece with its flocks of gold."
When thus he had spoken, Jason cast off
  his saffron robe, and trusting to god,
began the task. He did not waver before the fire,

by grace of the foreign enchantress's commands,
but seizing the plow, he bound the bulls' necks
to the gear, forcefully, and into their sturdy sides
drove the unwearying goad, and so the strong
hero worked to the end the measure
of his appointed task. Aietes, though speechless, shrieked
in astonishment at his strength. (231–3

Counter-turn 11

His comrades stretched forth to the stalwart man
their hands and crowned him with garlands
of grass and with gentle words
greeted him fondly. At once Helios'
wondrous son told of the shining hide,
where Phrixos' knives had flayed and stretched it.
He hoped that Jason would not achieve that too,
for it lay in a thicket and clung to
the most ravenous jaws of a snake,
which surpassed in length and breadth a fifty-oared ship,
fashioned by blows of iron. (239–

Stand 11

Long is my journey down the highway. The hour
closes in, and I know
a short path. To many others I am
a leader of skill in song.
He killed with cunning that green-eyed snake of spangled back,
Arkesilas, and stole a willing Medea,
the death of Pelias.
They encountered Okeanos' open main, the blushing sea,
and the race of Lemnian women who murdered their men.
There they contested in Thoas' funeral games,
with a garment for prize (247–

Turn 12

and shared the women's beds. In foreign fields
at that time the fateful day or watcher of night
received the seed
of your gleaming prosperity. There the race of
Euphamos, planted, flourished
forever after. Sharing the haunts of Lakedaimonian
men, they settled in time upon the isle
of Kalliste. From there the son
of Leto offered the plain of Libya

for you with the favor of gods to cultivate
and the divine city of golden-throned
Kyrene to administrate, *(254–61)*

Counter-turn 12 finding for it device of counseling right.
Know now the wisdom of Oidipous. For if
    a man with keen-cutting ax were to hack
the branches from a mighty oak and distort
    its marvelous form,
though failed of fruit, it would give account,
if ever it came at last to a winter's fire,
or propped upon the upright
    columns of some lord,
it performs wretched labor in alien walls,
having left bereft its own place. *(262–69)*

Stand 12 You are a healer most in season, and Paian
    honors your light.
One must apply a gentle hand to attend
    the trauma of a wound.
It is easy for the feeble to shake a city
but difficult to set it in place again,
    unless suddenly
god becomes a pilot to its leaders of men.
For you the grace of these things weaves to the end.
Only endure to show for blessed Kyrene
    all fervent concern. *(270–76)*

Turn 13 Of Homer's verse understand and cherish
this word: a good messenger, he said,
    brings greatest honor to every deed;
even the Muse is increased through correct
    report. Kyrene knew
and the most illustrious palace of Battos
the righteous mind of Damophilos. He, a youth among boys,
in counsel an elder who has achieved
    a hundred years of life,
orphans an evil tongue of conspicuous voice
and has learned to hate the violent man, *(277–84)*

Counter-turn 13 neither contending with noble men,
nor delaying any end. The critical hour

at the hands of men has brief measure.
This he has learned well. As a squire,
and not a slave, it follows him. They say
that this is most vile of all, to know the good
but by necessity to be without. Atlas indeed
wrestles now with heaven apart from his
possessions and native land.
Imperishable Zeus loosed the Titans. In time
there are shiftings of sails as the breeze (285–

Stand 13 abates. He prays that having drunk
to the dregs his deadly disease,
he will see his home again, and at Apollo's
spring, attending festivities,
give often his soul to youth, and among skilled
citizens, lifting his intricate lyre,
touch upon peace,
offering pain to none and suffering not at his townsmen's hands.
And perhaps he will tell, Arkesilas, what kind
of fountain he found of ambrosial words,
when lately a guest at Thebes. (293–

Pythian IX

For Telesikrates of Kyrene
Winner in the Footrace in Full Armor, 474 B.C.

Turn 1

I wish with the full-breasted Graces
to proclaim Telesikrates, of brazen shield
and victor at Pytho, a blessed man,
the garland of chariot-driving Kyrene,
whom once the long-haired son of Leto
    snatched from the hollows of Pelion
echoing with the wind; on golden car he bore
the untamed maid and made her there
queen of a land abundant in flocks and fruit,
to inhabit the lovely flourishing
    third root of a continent. *(1–8)*

Counter-turn 1

Silver-footed Aphrodite gave welcome to
the Delian guest and touched
with delicate hand the god-built chariot.
And upon their sweet bed she cast lovely modesty
and so arranged the god's marriage with
    the daughter of Hypseus, wide in strength,
who was at that time king of the overweening Lapithai,
a hero in generation second
from Okeanos, whom once in the famed vales of Pindos
the naiad Kreoisa, delighting in the bed
of Peneios, bore, *(9–16)*

Stand 1

the daughter of Earth. And Hypseus cherished
his child of the beautiful arms, Kyrene,
    who did not care to pace before the loom,
nor to delight in feasts with companions at home,
but with brazen javelins
and battling with sword to slay savage
beasts and so afford to her father's kine
a deep and restful peace,
    while she wasted upon her lids

scant sleep, that sweet companion
of bed as the dawn weighs near. (17–25

Turn 2

The Far-archer, wide-quivered Apollo,
came upon her once without her spears
and wrestling with an enormous lion.
Straightway he called Chiron from his halls and said,
"Abandon your sacred cave, O son of Philyra;
    marvel at a woman's spirit and mighty
strength, the battles she wages undauntedly,
a maiden with heart
surpassing toil. Her wits are not storm-tossed by fear.
Who of mortals bore her? From what stock
    has she been spawned (26–3

Counter-turn 2

"that she keeps the hollows of shadowy mountains
and tastes unbounded strength?
Is it right to lay my famed hand upon her
and in her bed to shear her honey-sweet meadow grass?"
Kentauros, inspired, smiling like springtime,
    with benign brow, straightway
gave his advice: "Hidden are the keys of wise
persuasion unlocking the holiest loves,
Phoibos, and modesty prevents men and gods alike
from approaching openly for the first time
    the sweetness of the marriage bed. (34–4

Stand 2

"For you, whom right does not permit to touch
upon a lie, your pleasant mood has beguiled
    to tease like this. Do you ask whence
the race of this maiden, O lord? You who know
the appointed end of all and all its paths,
how many leaves the earth puts forth in spring,
how many sands in rivers and sea
are driven by blasts of wave and wind
    and what will be and whence
it will come—this you see well.
But if I must match myself with the wise, (42–

Turn 3

"I will speak. You have come to this wooded glen
as husband to her and you shall carry her across
the sea to a choice garden of Zeus.

There you shall make her a city's queen, gathering
the island people about the plain-surrounded hill.
    And now the lady of spreading meadows, Libya,
will receive your glorious bride in golden halls,
welcomingly. And she will offer her a portion
of earth to be her lawful own,
not without tribute of fruit of every kind
nor unfamiliar with prey for the chase. *(51–58)*

Counter-turn 3

"There she shall have a child, whom famed Hermes
shall take from its own mother and bear
to the Hours, beautifully throned, and Earth.
Marveling at the babe upon their knees,
they shall distill upon its lips nectar
    and ambrosia, and make it immortal,
a Zeus, a holy Apollo, a joy to friendly men,
and constant guardian of flocks,
Agreus and Nomios, to some Aristaios by name."
So he spoke and prepared to sanction
    the wedding's sweet accomplishment. *(59–66)*

Stand 3

Swift, when the gods are set on haste,
is the deed, and short the paths. That day
determined all. They married in Libya's
gold-bedecked hall, where she tends a city
exceedingly beautiful and famed for games.
And now in very holy Pytho Karneiadas'
son has brought her blossoming fortune, for,
victorious there, he made Kyrene bright,
    and she will welcome him kindly
as he brings his lovely glory from Delphi
    to his homeland of beautiful women. *(67–75)*

Turn 4

Mighty deeds of valor have stories in plenty.
To embroider slight themes among the great
gives hearing to the skilled. Timeliness is crest
of everything alike. Seven-gated Thebes
learned once that Iolaos did not dishonor this. Him,
    when he had shorn with his sword
Eurystheus' head, they buried beneath the earth
    beside the tomb of the charioteer,

Amphitryon, where his father's father, guest of the Spartoi,
lay. He came to dwell in Kadmeian streets of white steeds. (76–8

Counter-turn 4

Married to him and to Zeus prudent
Alkmena in single labor bore
the battle-conquering strength of two sons.
Dull the man who does not lend his tongue to Herakles
and remembers not forevermore Dirkaion waters, which
    nourished him and Iphikles.
In fulfillment of my vow, I will celebrate them
    for favor received. May the clear light
of the sounding Graces not abandon me. At Aigina,
I say, and on Nisos' hill, thrice have I praised this city, (83–9

Stand 4

and so escaped the helplessness of silence.
And so, whether a citizen be friend or foe, let him
    not conceal what is worked for the common weal
and controvert the word of the old man of the sea,
who bade us praise even the foe,
with justice heartfelt, should he do good.
Often in the annual rites of Pelias
young girls have seen you win and silently,
    each to herself, wished that you
were her cherished husband
or son, O Telesikrates, (92–1

Turn 5

and in the Olympian games and those
of deep-bosomed Earth and in all those
of your native land. But as I quench my thirst
for song, someone exacts a debt from me,
the waking again of his ancestors' ancient glory:
    how for the sake of a Libyan woman
they went to the city Irasa, as suitors for Antaios'
famed daughter of the lovely hair,
whom many noble kin were courting
and many strangers too,
    since she was a beauty (101-

Counter-turn 5

to behold, and they wanted to pluck
the blossoming fruit of gold-garlanded
Hebe. But her father, cultivating for her
a more illustrious marriage, had heard how once

in Argos Danaos had found for forty-eight
    daughters before the noon of day
the swiftest of marriages. All the suitors he stood
straightway at the bounds of the race.
In contests of foot he bade them decide
whom each of the heroes who wished to be
    bridegrooms would have. *(109–16)*

Stand 5 And thus did the Libyan offer, wedding to his daughter
a husband. He stationed her at the goal
    to be the ultimate prize,
and in their midst he said that whoever first should spring
and touch her dress would take her home.
There Alexidamos, when he had nimbly finished the course,
took the cherished girl by the hand
and led her through the throng of Nomad horsemen.
    Many leaves did they fling
upon him and garlands too.
Many wings of victory had he accepted before. *(117–25)*

Nemean I

For Chromios of Aitna
Winner in the Chariot Race, 476(?) B.C.

Turn 1

Revered isle where Alpheus breathes again,
burgeoning branch of famous Syracuse, Ortygia,
bed of Artemis,
sister of Delos, from you the sweet-voiced
song rushes to bestow
enormous praise upon
    wind-hoofed horses, by grace of Aitnaian Zeus.
Chromios' chariot and Nemea compel me
    to yoke melody of praise to victorious deeds. (1–7)

Counter-turn 1

Beginnings are cast by the gods
with that man's inspired excellence.
In good fortune lies
the crown of reputation. The Muse is wont
to remember great games.
Now sow seed of glory
    upon the isle which Zeus, the lord
of Olympos, gave Persephone, and nodded
    his locks, queen of the fruitful earth, (8–14

Stand 1

fertile Sicily, to govern
    with its cities' crested opulence.
The son of Koronos provided that
    her people of horse and spear,
wooer of brazen war, be often wed
    with the golden leaves of Olympia's
olive wreaths. I have mounted
    with no false word the choice of many themes. (15–

Turn 2

I stand at the courtyard doors
of a hospitable man, singing beautifully,
where an appropriate feast
has been prepared for me, a house often

familiar to foreigners from
abroad; his fortune it is to have
noble friends to treat his slanderers
as water does smoke. Different men have different skills.
Treading a straight path one must strive with native talent. (19–25)

Counter-turn 2
Strength is proved in action,
and intelligence in counsel, for those in whom
it is inborn to see the future.
Son of Agesidamos, your character
includes this talent and that.
I do not love to keep
and conceal great wealth in my house
but to live well from my sufficiency
and acquire from friends good repute. Common the hopes (26–32)

Stand 2
of toil-worn men. I happily embrace
with my heart Herakles,
amidst these towering feats of excellence,
stirring the ancient story
of how as he came straightway from
his mother's womb to the wondrous light,
the child of Zeus, with his brother,
a twin from her labor— (33–36)

Turn 3
how, not escaping Hera, the golden-enthroned,
he was wrapped in saffron swaddling clothes,
but the queen of gods
in the haste of her wrath sent snakes straightway,
which, as the doors opened,
entered the spacious innermost room,
raging to embrace the babes
with ravenous jaws. But the hero
lifted his head to make first trial of battle (37–43)

Counter-turn 3
and grasped by their necks the two snakes
with his two inescapable hands.
And as he throttled them, time
breathed the life from their indescribable coils.
Unendurable fear
struck the women who attended Alkmena's bed,

for she herself leapt, barefoot, from her coverlet
and tried to ward off the monsters' attack. (44–50

Stand 3
Immediately Kadmeian chiefs
with weapons of bronze ran in throngs,
and brandishing in his hand a sword
bared from its scabbard,
Amphitryon came, stricken with piercing anguish.
His own pain presses everyone alike.
Straightway the heart is healed
of another's sorrow. (51–54

Turn 4
There he stood, overcome with wonder
and rapture alike, for he saw
the extraordinary spirit and strength
of his son. The immortals had made
reversed the messenger's report.
He called upon his neighbor,
distinguished prophet of exalted Zeus,
the infallible seer Teiresias, who told him
and all the host the child's adventures to come, (55–61

Counter-turn 4
how many monsters untamed
he would slay on land and on sea,
and to one walking
with slanted satiety, most despicable of men,
he foretold he would deal death.
For when the gods on Phlegra's plain
should encounter the giants in battle,
by Herakles' shafts their shining hair
would be befouled by the dust of earth. (62–6

Stand 4
So he spoke. But the hero himself
at rest forevermore should have
as his lot in choice requital for
his enormous toils peace
in opulent halls, receiving Hebe
as his blossoming bride and keeping
the marriage feast beside the son of Kronos
in praise of the solemn rite. (69–7

Nemean III

For Aristokleides of Aigina
Winner in the Pankration, 475(?) B.C.

Turn 1
O revered Muse, our mother, I beg you,
in the sacred month of the Nemean games, come
to Aigina, the Dorian isle of hospitality. For beside
Asopian waters await youthful architects
of honey-tongued triumph songs, craving your voice.
Different deeds thirst for different recompense,
but victory at the games loves song especially,
the most befitting attendant of wreaths and excellence. (1–8)

Counter-turn 1
Of my skill grant ungrudgingness.
Begin for the king of the cloud-enshrouded sky,
O his daughter, an esteemed song, and I shall share it
with their voices and lyre. It will be a charming task,
adornment of the land where formerly the Myrmidons
dwelt. Their meeting place of ancient fame
Aristokleides did not, by your favor, stain
with proof of softness amid the exceedingly strong (9–16)

Stand 1
pankration host. In Nemea's deep plain
as a healthful remedy for his wearisome blows
    he took a lovely victory.
And if, handsome, he achieved what befitted his form,
and entered upon manhood's height,
    Aristophanes' child, no further with ease
could he cross untrodden seas beyond the pillars of Herakles, (17–21)

Turn 2
which that hero and god established as famed
and final witnesses of voyaging. He overcame on the sea's main
monstrous beasts, and alone he tracked the rivulet shoals
until he reached the goal that sent him home again,
and he made known the land. My soul, to what foreign
promontory do you divert my voyaging course?
For Aiakos and his race I bid you bring the Muse.
The blossom of justice attends the word, "Praise the good," (22–29)

Counter-turn 2

nor is passion for others' possessions better for man.
Hunt at home. Your lot, a becoming ornament,
is to sing something sweet. In ancient excellence
King Peleus rejoiced. Cleaving an oversize spear,
he took Iolkos, alone, without a host,
and grasped Thetis, the sea nymph,
vigorously. And Telamon, broad in strength,
Iolaos' companion, destroyed Laomedon. (30–3

Stand 2

And he followed him once against the bronze-bowed
strength of Amazons, nor ever did quelling terror
    blunt the edge of his wits.
With glory inborn a man has great weight,
but he who is taught, lives in obscurity. With constant
    changes of breath, he never puts a foot secure,
but with unfinished mind tastes of myriad arts. (38–4

Turn 3

Blond Achilles, while still in Philyra's house,
a little child, played at mighty deeds, and often brandished
in his hands a tiny javelin, swift as the winds.
In battle he slaughtered savage lions and slew
wild boars, and lugged their heaving carcasses
back to Kentauros, son of Kronos,
at first, when six years old, and then forever after.
Artemis and bold Athena marveled at him (43–

Counter-turn 3

slaying deer without hounds or deceptive nets.
He had power of foot. I tell a story told by men
who lived before. The wise Chiron nurtured Jason
in his rocky cave, and afterward Asklepios,
whom he taught the gentle-handed lore of medicine.
Again, he married to Peleus Nereus' daughter
of gleaming breasts and cherished for her their brave son,
swelling his soul with every appropriate thing (51–

Stand 3

so that, when sped by the sea's blasts of wind, he came
beneath the walls of Troy, he should endure the Lykian clash of
        spears
    and their battle cry; the Phrygians'
and Dardanians' too; and encountering spear-
bearing Aithiopians, he might fix it

in his soul, that their king should not return
home again, Memmon, the inspired kin of Helenos. *(59–63)*

Turn 4 And so the light, shining afar, is fixed for Aiakidai.
For yours is their blood, Zeus, yours the contest for which
my song celebrates with voice of youths the land's delight.
That cry befits the victor Aristokleides,
who linked this isle to glorious account
and to splendid concerns the Pythian's
sacred Thearion. In attempt the end
shines through wherever one is superior, *(64–71)*

Counter-turn 4 as a boy among young boys, as a man among men,
or third, among the elders, whatever portion we have,
our mortal race. Human life drives on
fourfold excellence, urging concern for the thing at hand.
In this you do not fail. Farewell, my friend. To you
I send this strain of honey mixed with snowy white
milk, the foam of its mingling upon it,
a drink of song with Aiolian breath of flutes, *(72–79)*

Stand 4 late though it be. Among birds the eagle is swift.
He snatches with speed, as he swoops from afar,
his bloody prey in his claws.
Chattering jackdaws range far below.
Upon you, by grace of Klio, beautifully throned,
because of your winning resolve,
from Nemea and Epidauros, from Megara too, the light has shown. *(80–84)*

Threnos VII, Frs. 130–34

For those below there shines in its strength
the sun while here it is night.
In meadows red with roses
the forecourt of their city
is shadowed by boughs of frankincense
and burdened with gold-fruited trees.
Here they delight in horses and contests
of sport; there in games of chess and the lyre.
All flowering bliss blooms for them there.
A lovely fragrance drifts over the land
as ever they mingle all manner of sacrifice
with flame that blazes afar upon
the altars of the gods . . .

Blessed all those who by
allotted destiny
of toil-releasing ritual . . .

The body of every man is attendant upon
death of excessive strength,
but there remains alive a phantom
    of life, which is alone
from the gods. It sleeps while the limbs act,
but for men who sleep, in many dreams,
it presents prescient perception
of what will be delicious or difficult.

The souls of those from whom Persephone
shall accept recompense of ancient sorrow
she shall, in the ninth year, send back
to the sun above. From these there shall grow
noble kings and men swift in strength
and in wisdom superior. For all remaining time
they are named sacred heroes by mortal men.

The happiness of the blessed is not a fugitive.

LIST OF POETS

NOTES

GLOSSARY OF PROPER NAMES

SELECT BIBLIOGRAPHY

LIST OF POETS

Alkaios: Of Mytilene on the island Lesbos. Late seventh–early sixth century B.C. An aristocrat, he allied himself with Pittakos against the tyrant Myrsilos. Pittakos seems later to have gone over to Myrsilos, and Alkaios accordingly reviles him in many of his poems. Alkaios was in exile upon more than one occasion and is known to have gone to Egypt. He wrote love poems, hymns, and drinking songs as well as political poems.

Alkman: Probably a native Spartan, though in antiquity it was disputed whether he was a native Spartan or an immigrant from Lydia and even whether he was born free or as a slave. He wrote maiden songs for choruses of young girls. Because he often wrote about food he acquired in antiquity a reputation as a glutton.

Anakreon: Originally from Teos in Asia Minor. Driven from there by the Persian incursions, he settled in Thrace and died perhaps in Athens. He lived ca. 560–490 B.C.

Archilochos: Born about 680 B.C. on the island of Paros but later, perhaps between 660 and 650 B.C., went with a second wave of settlers to Thasos, which his father, Telesikles, had helped to colonize a generation earlier. The gossip in antiquity was that Lykambes had promised his daughter Neoboule to him in marriage but later changed his mind. In retaliation Archilochos wrote such savage verses against him and his daughters that they all hanged themselves. He is reported to have died fighting in about 640 B.C.

Bakchylides: Nephew of Simonides. Contemporary of Pindar, whose dates are 518–ca. 440 B.C. Wrote dithyrambs, paians, and odes of great charm for the victors in the games.

Hipponax: Lived at Ephesos, Asia Minor, in the sixth century B.C.

Ibykos: Born probably at Rhegion, a Greek settlement in Italy. Worked in the latter half of the sixth century B.C. Traveled about the Greek world as a professional choral poet.

Kallinos: Lived in Ephesos, Asia Minor, in the middle of the seventh century B.C. His poem may be about the Kimmerian invasion of Ionia.

Korinna: Of Tanagra or possibly Thebes in Boiotia. Probably an older contemporary of Pindar. An anecdote from antiquity tells us that she criticized Pindar for not using myths in his poems, and when he composed a poem mentioning eight myths in six lines, she laughed and said that he should sow with the hand, not the sack. She writes in her native dialect and about Boiotian myths that are peculiarly primitive.

Mimnermos: Lived at Kolophon in Asia Minor. Late seventh–early sixth century B.C. Was known in antiquity for his love poems, especially for a woman named Nanno, but fragments of his poetry show that he dealt with other subjects as well, including mythology, history, and warfare.

Pindar: Of Thebes. Lived from 518–ca. 440 B.C. A professional poet, he traveled widely, to Sicily and perhaps to Libya as well as all about Greece. The tyrant Hiero of Syracuse was one of his patrons. Although fragments of other works (dithyrambs, paians, threnoi) survive, he is famous for his four books of victory odes, which are unsurpassed for their diaphanous beauty.

Praxilla: Of Sikyon. She wrote hymns, a dithyramb *Achilles*, and drinking songs. Fifth century B.C. Only a few fragments survive.

Sappho: Of Mytilene on the island Lesbos. Late seventh, early sixth century B.C. She had a circle of young women to whom she wrote love lyrics and for whose marriages she wrote wedding songs. Antiquity regarded her as the greatest of the lyric poets. She is said to have married and to have had a daughter, Kleïs, to whom some of her poems are addressed.

Semonides: Lived on the small Aegean island of Amorgos. Date uncertain but perhaps late seventh century B.C.

Simonides: Of the Aegean island Keos. Lived 556–468 B.C. As a professional poet he traveled all over Greece and seems to have been equally at home in Athens or Sparta. He wrote dirges, hymns, elegies, inscriptional epigrams, drinking songs, encomia, as well as the famous lullaby of Danae to Perseus.

Solon: The famous Athenian statesman, ca. 630–550 B.C. Archon in 594/3 B.C. One of the Seven Wise Men of the ancient world. He set forth his very influential political and moral views in his poetry.

Stesichoros: A professional choral poet from southern Italy or Sicily. Worked in the early or middle sixth century B.C. He treated mythological or epic themes in long choral poems, such as his *Oresteia*, *Helen*, and *Tale of Geryon*, and these had a great influence upon the vase painters and the Attic tragedians.

Theognis: From Megara. Lived in the middle or later sixth and perhaps into the fifth century B.C. Much of his poetry, addressed to his friend Kyrnos, inveighs against the rise of the merchant class.

Tyrtaios: Worked at Sparta, probably in the late seventh century B.C. May have been a Spartan, an Athenian, or a Milesian.

NOTES

Homeric Hymns

II. *Hymn to Demeter*: May date to the first half of the seventh century B.C. The poem appears to contain allusions to the Eleusinian mysteries.

IV. *Hymn to Hermes*: May date to the middle of the seventh century B.C. A megaron is a cave, a hall, or a palace.

V. *Hymn to Aphrodite*: Probably dates to about 700 B.C.

VI. *Hymn to Aphrodite*: Date unknown but seems to be neither very early nor very late. Author may have been a Kyprian. Orichalc is mountain copper, used in antiquity for mirrors.

VII. *Hymn to Dionysos*: Date is probably not later than the sixth century B.C.

XXVIII. *Hymn to Athena*: May date to the fifth century B.C., but the agitation of nature at the birth of the goddess seems archaic in spirit.

Archilochos

12. The "grievous gifts" are corpses.

23. No one knows the significance of "I am an Ant." The entire fragment is in fact a puzzle.

105. Herakleitos, *Homeric Allegories*, to whom we owe this poem, says: ". . . just as Archilochos, entangled in the Thracian troubles, likens the war to a storm at sea, somehow thus . . ." (translation Edmonds).

122. Aristotle in his *Rhetoric* tells us that this is the astonished response of a father whose unattractive daughter had received a proposal of marriage. Actually, it seems to describe an eclipse of the sun on 5 April 647, or possibly on 27 June 660 B.C.

174, 176, 177, 178, 185, 187. Seem to be from one or more animal fables.

185. A messenger-stick was a staff around which a message was written in such a way that unwound it was unintelligible. The recipient had to wind it around a similar staff to read it. It was a way of sending secret dispatches.

196a. This papyrus fragment was found in a mummy at Cologne in 1973.

223. Archilochos addresses a critic: he is like a cricket who will sing (i.e., criticize) even more loudly when caught by the wing.

325, 326, 330, 331. Considered spurious by West.

Hipponax

115. This poem has traditionally been ascribed to Archilochos. I follow West in attributing it to Hipponax.

Alkman

1. From a papyrus found at Saqqâra in 1855. The earlier part, which is extremely fragmentary, deals with an obscure myth. The lines I translate begin at line 35 and break off at 101, four lines before the end of the poem. Girls in a chorus seem to sing of themselves as rivals of a second chorus (the Peleiades) and to compare themselves for beauty and grace of movement to racehorses.

16. This fragment was used in antiquity to "prove" Alkman's Lydian origin.

26. The ancient source for this poem, Antigonos of Karystos, in his *Marvels*, says: "Male halcyons are called ceryli. When they become weak from old age and are no longer able to fly, the females carry them, taking them on their wings. What Alkman says is connected with this: weak from old age and unable to whirl about with the choirs and the girls' dancing, he says . . ." (translation Campbell). The halcyon, a semimythical bird, is often identified with the European kingfisher. I have translated "cerylos" as "halcyon" and "halcyons" as "kingfishers."

56. To a maenad, a female worshipper of Dionysos, who was supposed to have the power of milking lionesses. Argeïphontes (Hermes) was represented in art as carrying the infant Dionysos to heaven.

59b. Athenaios, *Doctors at Dinner*, says of this fragment, "And he [Alkman] speaks as having fallen wildly in love with Megalostrata, a poetess but able to attract her lovers by her conversation" (translation Campbell).

60. A girl or a girls' chorus is probably addressing Hera.

79. The subject is Tantalos.

81. Nausikaa, the princess who befriended Odysseus, addresses her companions.

Stesichoros

178. From the *Funeral Games for Pelias*. Hermes and Hera gave these horses to Kastor and Polydeukes.

179 a and b. Also from the *Funeral Games for Pelias*. May describe a wedding, perhaps that of Alkestis, Pelias' daughter, to Admetos, one of the competitors in the chariot race.

180. From the *Funeral Games for Pelias*. Probably describes a boxing-thong.

181, 184, 185. From the *Tale of Geryon*, Herakles' adventures in the West as he went to capture the cattle of Geryon.

186. Refers to the monster Geryon.

187. From the *Helen*. This fragment probably describes the wedding of Helen and Menelaos.

188. Also from the *Helen*.

192. From the *Palinode*. The ancient story was that Stesichoros was struck blind for having slandered Helen in his *Helen*. After writing this recantation his sight was restored.

200. Athena, the daughter of Zeus, pities Epeios, the builder of the wooden horse. From the *Sack of Troy*.

210, 211, 212. From Stesichoros' *Oresteia* (*Tale of Orestes*).

219. Also from the *Oresteia*. The passage appears to refer to Klytemnestra's dream, but it is uncertain whether the "king of the Pleisthenid line" is Agamemnon or Orestes.

221. From the *Boar-Hunters*. This poem may have been about the famous Kalydonian boar hunt.

223. Perhaps from the *Helen*.

S 15. A recently discovered papyrus describing two of the labors of Herakles: the slaying of the Lernaian Hydra and of Geryon.

Ibykos

321. Refers to the building of the bridge joining of the island Ortygia to the mainland of Sicily. This was done in the middle of the sixth century B.C. and so was new in Ibykos' time.

Sappho

1. The only complete poem we have from Sappho. Dionysios of Halikarnassos quoted it for its polished style and said of it: "The euphony and charm of this passage lie in the cohesion and smoothness of the joinery. Words are juxtaposed and interwoven according to certain natural affinities and groupings of the letters" (translation Campbell).

2. Found inscribed on a potsherd of the third century B.C. I have supplied "from good bees" to fill out the line.

Alkaios

69. The "holy city" may be Mytilene. "He, like a crafty fox" may refer to Pittakos.

73. The fragment may be either a political or an erotic metaphor.

119. This too may be either political or erotic in meaning.

130b. Alkaios writes as a political exile.

140. The armor Alkaios describes is distinctly old-fashioned. He seems to describe it for present inspiration.

208. The ancient critic Herakleitos, in his *Homeric Allegories*, tells us that this poem is a political allegory and refers to the tyrannical conspiracy of Myrsilos.

350 a and b. To his brother Antimenidas, who had served as a mercenary with the Babylonian army.

Anakreon

341, fr. 1. The line "Herotima, you public thoroughfare" may be the beginning of another poem.

347. "I hear the notorious woman" may begin a new poem.

348. Addressed to Artemis.

374. The magadis was an instrument of twenty strings arranged in octaves.

388. "Wasped cap" may refer to a hood tied tightly or to some kind of hairstyle.

423a. "Solecian" means "barbarian" according to the ancient source, Herodian, *On Non-Greek Words and Solecisms.*

458. Clement of Alexandria, *The Schoolmaster*, the source for this fragment, says, "Womanish movements and pampered and luxurious habits are to be cut out completely; for effeminacy of movement in walking and 'going along with hips swaying,' as Anakreon puts it, are thoroughly meretricious" (translation Campbell).

Simonides

509. From a victory song for Glaukos of Karystos.

515. Aristotle, *Rhetoric*, writes: "Once when Simonides was offered too small a fee by the victor in the mule race, he refused to write him an ode, on the plea that he could not bring himself to write in honour of mules. But when he offered him sufficient pay, he took it and wrote: 'Hail, ye daughters of storm-footed steeds!' And yet they were also daughters of asses" (translation Edmonds).

550a. This means that the sail was dyed crimson with the insect *kokkos*, which, dried, yields a dye of a red-purple color. The ancients thought that the insect was a "blossom" of the kermes oak. *Kokkos* means "berry."

567. This fragment is about Orpheus.

575. The child is Eros (Love).

639. This is quoted by Herodian, *On Solecisms*, to show that Simonides incorrectly used a first-person pronoun with a third-person verb.

Korinna

654. Lines 1–12, 32–52 of column 1, all but a few words of column 2, lines 1–11 of column 3, and virtually all of column 4 of this poem are miss-

ing from the papyrus. The two fragments we have were therefore widely separated in the original poem and the connection between them is obscure. Both, however, deal with local Boiotian myths that are otherwise unknown to us.

Praxilla

747. From a hymn to Adonis.

748. From the dithyramb *Achilles.*

749. A drinking song, sometimes included among the Attic skolia (drinking songs) and not attributed to Praxilla.

Anonymous

892–901. Drinking songs. Nos. 893–896 are often known as the tyrant-fighter songs.

848. This is a children's "trick-or-treat" song from Rhodes.

852. A children's play song.

869. A work song, no doubt obscene.

902, 904. Drinking songs.

Bakchylides

Epinician III: This poem praises Hiero for the generosity of his offerings at Delphi by reminding him of how Apollo rescued Kroisos from his funeral pyre and transported him to the fabled land of the Hyperboreans in return for his gifts to Delphi. Kroisos was a historical figure and Sardis did fall to the Persians in 546 B.C. Herodotos 1.86ff. gives another version of the same story.

Epinician V: It is difficult to see how this melancholy tale of Oineus' death from Artemis' wrath, Meleager's death at the agency of his mother, and the presaging of Herakles' death at the hands of Deianeira can have been of much cheer to Hiero, who is known to have been ill at this time. He suffered from the stone. Perhaps the point is simply that no one on earth, not even Hiero, is blessed in every respect.

Epinician XIII: The poem begins, as we have it (the first 44 lines are lost), with a reference to Herakles' slaying of the Nemean lion at the site of the present victory; tells next of Pytheas' return to Aigina, home of Endaïs, wife of Aiakos, who bore Peleus and Telamon, fathers of Achilles and Ajax; this leads to an account, taken from the *Iliad*, of Hektor's attempt to fire the Greek ships at Troy while Achilles in his wrath refrained from battle. The pankration was a contest that combined wrestling and boxing.

Dithyramb XVI: This poem tells the story, known also from Sophokles' *Women of Trachis*, of Herakles' sack of Oichalia and of his bringing home as his bride the princess Iole, and hints at Deianeira's slaying of Herakles by the shirt she innocently poisons with Nessos' so-called love charm.

Dithyramb XVII: This poem tells of a quarrel between Theseus, the Athenian, and Minos, the Cretan, aboard the ship that carried fourteen Athenian victims to the Cretan Minotaur, over Minos' touching the cheek of the Athenian maiden Eriboia. Theseus boasts that he is the son of Poseidon and Minos that his father is Zeus himself. Zeus makes good Minos' claim by a flash of lightning, and Theseus accepts Minos' challenge to retrieve a golden ring from the deep. He succeeds and so proves his paternity too.

Dithyramb XVIII: This poem, which tells of Theseus' coming to Athens, mentions his slaying of several notorious villains.

Paian IV: This is the last of three fragments belonging to a hymn of praise to Apollo. It tells of the pleasure of peace.

Paian VI: This is all that remains of this poem.

Pindar

Olympian I: This ode tells of Pelops' winning of his bride Hippodameia in the chariot race at Pisa, which was the true beginning of the Olympian contests. Pindar eschews the story of Tantalos' cannibal feast of Pelops to the gods. Tantalos' sin was rather the offering of nectar and ambrosia to mortals.

Olympian VI: The victor Hagesias, originally of Stymphalos in Arkadia, was from the noble family of the Iamidai, hereditary prophets and diviners at the great altar of Zeus at Olympia. This ode therefore tells of the birth of Iamos, the ancestor of the Iamidai. On "letter-staff" see note on Archilochos 185.

Olympian VII: The myth in this ode is told in reverse sequence. The chronological order is as follows: 1. Helios, absent at the original partitioning of the earth, was in the end awarded the island Rhodes, bride of Helios (the Sun). 2. Helios' sons, bidden to raise an altar to Athena and Zeus, forgot fire and offered flameless sacrifices. Nevertheless, Zeus granted the Rhodians gold; and Athena, craft. 3. Tlapolemos slew Likymnios, but Apollo sent him to Rhodes, where he received "sweet requital for piteous disaster."

Olympian XIII: This ode begins with the praise of Corinth, a city of great inventors; moves on to praise the Corinthian victor Xenophon; then tells the story of Bellerophon, who with Athena's help "discovered" the bridle to ride his winged horse, Pegasos; and ends with praise of Xenophon's clan, the Oligaïthidai. The stade was a track for footraces; also a standard measure of distance equal to about 607 feet.

Pythian I: Pindar is here concerned with Hiero's foundation of the city of Aitna near Mount Aitna and his establishment there of his son Deinomenes as king. The ode is memorable for its description of the monster Typho, who, as an example of those whom Zeus loves not, lies in Tartaros, pinned beneath Mount Aitna in Sicily and the shores of Kyme (Cumae) in Italy. The poet tells of Philoktetes, who suffered from a festering foot, and hopes that Hiero, who was also ailing, will have equal restoration. Pindar ends by comparing the victory of Hiero over the Carthaginians at Himera in 480 B.C. with the victories of the Athenians at Salamis in 480 B.C. and of the Spartans at Plataia in 479 B.C. over the Persians in 479 B.C., and by mentioning Hiero's victory over the Etruscans at Kyme in 474 B.C.

Pythian III: Pindar wishes that Chiron, the kindly centaur who had taught Asklepios the healing art, were alive today to help Hiero in his illness. He then tells of Asklepios' birth to Koronis, who had lain with Apollo and bore his seed but fell in love with an Arkadian stranger, Ischys, Eilatos' son. Apollo therefore sent Artemis to destroy Koronis, but he rescued his son Asklepios from Koronis' corpse as her coffin burned upon the funeral pyre. "The Mother" (line 78) is Rhea, a Phrygian goddess. Pindar had a chapel to her and to Pan in front of his house. The pentathlon was a contest of five events: short race, broad jump, discus, javelin, and wrestling.

Pythian IV: Damophilos of Kyrene, who had been banished by the king Arkesilas for participating in an aristocratic rebellion, commissioned his friend Pindar, upon the occasion of Arkesilas' victory, to write this ode, which ends with a plea to Arkesilas to restore Damophilos. The story it tells is that of the foundation of Kyrene as prophesied by Medea. This leads Pindar to tell the story of the Argonauts.

Pythian IX: This ode tells of Apollo's marriage to the nymph Kyrene and the foundation in Libya of the city Kyrene—the nymph and the city are scarcely separable here—and of the birth of their child, Aristaios. He ends by telling how Antaios solved the problem of the many Libyan suitors of his daughter: he remembered how Danaos had arranged a footrace to marry off his forty-eight daughters, and he did the same.

Nemean I: This ode tells of the birth of Herakles, mentions his labors and his requital in heaven with his bride Hebe.

Nemean III: This ode tells of the marriage of Peleus and Thetis and of Chiron's rearing of Achilles, Jason, and Asklepios. Pankration: see note on Bakchylides, *Epinician XIII*.

Threnos VII: A threnos is a lament for the dead. This fragment with its lovely and very unusual description of the underworld (most ancients, if they believed in it at all, thought it a very gloomy place) reveals that Pindar believed in the transmigration of souls.

GLOSSARY OF PROPER NAMES

Abanthis: A young woman of Sappho's circle.
Achaians: Homer's name for the Greeks in general.
Acheron: A river of the underworld.
Achilles: Son of Peleus and Thetis. The best Greek warrior at Troy.
Admetos: A king of Pherae in Thessaly, northern Greece, who allowed his wife to die for him. He was the son of Pheres, one of the Argonauts.
Adonis: A handsome youth with whom Aphrodite fell in love. Despite her pleas, he persisted in hunting and was killed by a boar. Originally a dying-and-rising fertility god, he was mourned annually.
Adrastos: A king of Argos. Driven out of his country by Amphiaraos.
Aegean Sea: The sea between Greece and Asia Minor.
Agamemnon: Son of Atreus. Brother of Menelaos. Husband of Klytemnestra.
Agelaos: Brother of Meleager.
Agesidamos: Father of the victor Chromios.
Agesilaidas: A friend of Alkaios.
Agido: A Spartan girl, apparently the second-in-command, after Hagesichora, leader of the chorus in Alkman 1.
Agreus: An epithet of Aristaios. Means "hunter."
Aiakidai: Descendants of Aiakos. The "fenced grove" thereof is Aigina, of which Aiakos was the founder.
Aiakos: The father of Peleus. Grandfather of Achilles.
Aidoneus: Hades, god of the underworld.
Aietes: Son of Helios. Father of Medea. King of Kolchis.
Aigai: A place in southern Euboia, the large island off central Greece.
Aigimios: Friend of Hyllos and ancestor of the Dorian race.
Aigina: An island off Attica, central Greece.
Aineas: Leader of the chorus in *Olympian VI.*
Aineias: Son of Aphrodite and Anchises. One of the important warriors of the Trojan War. In the *Hymn to Aphrodite* (V), Aphrodite claims to have named him from the word *ainos,* which means "terrible."
Ainesimbrota: A Spartan girl.
Ainos: A city of Thrace, northern Greece.
Aiolic: Aiolian.
Aiolian: Refers to the Greek tribe descended from Aiolos, a king of Thessaly. It is also the dialect of Sappho and Alkaios of Lesbos. In Alkaios 129 it means the "goddess of Aiolos" and probably refers to Hera.
Aiolid: Son of Aiolos, i.e., Sisyphos.

Aiolos: King of Thessaly and great-grandfather of Jason and Bellerophon.
Aipytos: Son of Eilatos. Adoptive father of Evadna, the mother by Apollo of Iamos.
Aisimidas: A friend of Alkaios.
Aison: Father of Jason.
Aithiopians: The Ethiopians of Africa.
Aithra: Daughter of Pittheus, king of Troezen. Wife of Aigeus, who was the grandfather of Theseus.
Aitna: A volcano of Sicily. Also the nearby city founded by Hiero.
Aitnaian: Refers to either the city or the volcano Aitna.
Aitolians: The people of Aitolia, a province of west-central Greece.
Ajax: 1. Son of Telamon of Salamis. After Achilles, the greatest Greek warrior at Troy. 2. Son of Oileus. The "lesser Ajax." A Greek warrior at Troy, who raped Kassandra.
Akeste: A nymph and playmate of Persephone. Daughter of Ocean and Tethys.
Akraiphen: The eponymous hero of the town Akraiphen of Boiotia. A prophet.
Alatas: Leader of the Dorian invasion of the Peloponnesos. Founder of Dorian power at Corinth. Pindar considers the Corinthians Alatas' descendants.
Alexidamos: Ancestor of the victor Telesikrates.
Alexis: An acquaintance of Anakreon.
Alkaïdai: Descendants of Alkaios, father of Amphitryon, Herakles' mortal father.
Alkibia: An acquaintance of Archilochos.
Alkman: The poet.
Alkmena: Wife of Amphytrion and mother by Zeus of Herakles.
Alpheus: A river of the Peloponnesos. Runs through Arkadia and Elis past Olympia.
Althaia: Mother of Meleager. To avenge her brothers whom Meleager had slain in a dispute over the Kalydonian boar's hide she killed Meleager by throwing into the fire the firebrand that, it had been prophesied, would end his life.
Alyattes: Father of Kroisos. King of Lydia, ca. 610–560 B.C.
Amalthea: The she-goat who nourished the infant Zeus. One of her horns flowed with nectar, the other with ambrosia.
Amazons: Female warriors who lived in the area of the Black Sea.
Amenas: A stream on which the city Aitna was built.
Ammon: A cult title of Zeus in Libya. Actually an Egyptian divinity whom the Greeks identified with Zeus.
Amphiaraos: A great prophet and hero of Argos in the Peloponnesos. One of the Seven against Thebes.
Amphimedo: Known only from Archilochos 196a. Presumably the

mother of the young girl to whom Archilochos here makes love.

Amphitrite: A sea nymph, wife of Poseidon.

Amphitryon: The mortal father of Herakles. Husband of Alkmena.

Amyklai: A town on the Eurotas, the river south of Sparta.

Amyntoridai: Descendants of Amyntor, father of Astydameia, the mother by Herakles of Tlapolemos.

Amythan: Brother of Aison, father of Melampos. One of the Argonauts.

Anaktoria: A young woman of Sappho's circle.

Anauros: A river of Thessaly, northern Greece.

Anchises: A distinguished Trojan. Consort of Aphrodite, who bore to him Aineias, one of the important warriors of the Trojan War.

Andromache: Wife of the Trojan hero Hektor.

Andromeda: A woman who appears to have been a rival of Sappho.

Ankaios: Brother of Meleager.

Antaios: 1. King of Irasa in Libya. 2. A giant. Son of Poseidon. King of Libya. Killed by Herakles.

Antron: A city of Thessaly, northern Greece.

Aphares: Althaia's brother. Meleager's uncle.

Aphrodite: Goddess of love. Daughter of Zeus and Dione. Mother of Aineias.

Apollo: Son of Zeus and Leto. Sister of Artemis. God of music, light, and healing.

Archilochos: The poet.

Ares: Son of Zeus and Hera. God of war.

Areta: A Spartan girl.

Arethousa: The spring of Ortygia, the island near Syracuse. Originally a daughter of Ocean and the nymph Arkadia, she was pursued by the river god Alpheus.

Argeïphontes: Hermes. The name means "slayer of Argos."

Argive: Of Argos.

Argo: The ship on which Jason and his crew sailed to fetch the golden fleece.

Argonauts: The company of men from all over Greece who accompanied Jason in his quest for the golden fleece.

Argos: A city in the northeast of the Peloponnesos. Sometimes refers to the surrounding district as well.

Aristaios: Son of Apollo and Kyrene.

Aristodemos: One of the Seven Wise Men of the ancient world.

Aristogeiton: An aristocratic Athenian who with Harmodios slew Hipparchos, brother of the tyrant Hippias in 514 B.C.

Aristokleides: 1. A friend of Anakreon. 2. The Aiginetan victor in the pankration at Nemea in 475(?) B.C.

Aristophanes: Father of the victor Aristokleides.

Aristophon: Apparently a hero of the island Naxos.

Arkadia: A province of the central Peloponnesos.
Arkesilas (IV): Son of Battos IV, king of Kyrene, victor in the chariot race at the Pythian games, 462 B.C.
Artemis: Virgin goddess of the hunt, childbirth, the moon. Sister of Apollo. Daughter of Zeus and Leto.
Artemon: A nouveau riche man pilloried by Anakreon.
Asia: The continent.
Asine: In Bakchylides, *Paian IV*, a town near Argos in the Peloponnesos.
Asklepios: Son of Zeus and Koronis. Chiron taught him the art of medicine. Zeus blasted him with a thunderbolt for having raised a mortal from the dead. Later a god of medicine.
Asopian: Of Asopos, the river of Boiotia.
Asopos: A river of Boiotia, central Greece.
Astaphis: A Spartan girl.
Astydameia: Mother by Herakles of Tlapolemos.
Astymeloisa: A Spartan girl, perhaps the choir leader in Alkman 3.
Atabyrion: The highest mountain on Rhodes. There was a temple of Zeus there.
Athena: Goddess of wisdom, crafts, warfare. Daughter of Zeus and Metis (Wise Counsel). Sprang fully armed from her father's head. Protectress of the city of Athens.
Athenian: Of Athens.
Athens: The chief city of Attica, central Greece.
Atlas: Brother of Prometheus. He made war with the other Titans against Zeus and so was condemned to bear heaven on his head and hands. Father of the Pleiades and the Hesperides.
Atreid: A descendant of Atreus. In Alkaios 70 it refers to Pittakos, who married into the house of the Penthilidai, who claimed descent from Orestes' son Penthilos. Orestes was a grandson of Atreus.
Atreus: Father of Agamemnon and Menelaos.
Atthis: A young woman of Sappho's circle.
Aulis: A city of Boiotia where the Greeks were detained on their way to Troy by contrary winds and so sacrificed Iphigenia.
Bacchant: A worshipper of Dionysos.
Bacchic: Refers to the worship of Dionysos.
Bassarids: Female worshippers of Dionysos.
Batousiades: An acquaintance of Archilochos.
Battos: A nickname said to mean "stutterer," given to Aristotoles, the colonizer of Libya. He was founder and first king of Kyrene.
Bellerophon: A Corinthian hero. Son of Glaukos. Tamer of the winged horse Pegasos, on which he attempted to fly to Olympos.
Blondie: The name of a horse (Xanthos) in Stesichoros 178.
Boibias: A lake of Thessaly in northern Greece.
Boiotian: Of Boiotia, a province of central Greece.
Boreas: The north wind.

Bowlegs: The name of a horse (Kyllaros) in Stesichoros 178.
Briseis: Achilles' concubine, whom Agamemnon took from him and so caused the wrath that gave the Trojans temporary advantage in the war.
Bykchis: A friend of Alkaios.
Carian: Of Caria, a country of Asia Minor.
Chalkidian: Of Chalkis, a city of Euboia, the large island off the west coast of central Greece.
Chariklo: Wife of the centaur Chiron.
Charilaos: A friend of Archilochos.
Charybdis: A dangerous whirlpool between Italy and Sicily.
Chimaira: Son of Typhon and Echidna, a triple-form monster.
Chiron: The wisest and noblest of the centaurs. Tutor to Achilles, Jason, Asklepios. Son of Kronos and Philyra. Lived on Mount Pelion in Thessaly, northern Greece.
Chopper: Prokoptes, elsewhere Prokrustes. He fitted his victims to his bed by chopping off the overlapping limbs of those who were too big and by hammering out those of the too-small.
Chromios: The Aitnaian victor in the chariot race at Nemea in 476(?) B.C.
Chryseis: A nymph and playmate of Persephone. Daughter of Ocean and Tethys.
Commander of Many: Hades.
Corinth: A city on the isthmus connecting the Peloponnesos to the rest of Greece.
Cretan: Refers to the island of Crete.
Crete: A large island in the Mediterranean Sea.
Cutter of Wood: Same as Undercutter, the worm that was believed to cause toothache.
Daïpylos: Father of Klymenos, one of the Kouretes of Aitolia.
Damagetos: Father of the victor Diagoras.
Damoanektides: A friend of Alkaios.
Damophilos: An exiled Kyrenian nobleman of democratic persuasion. He apparently asked Pindar to write *Pythian IV* to persuade Arkesilas to allow him to return to Kyrene.
Danaans: Homer's name for the Greeks in general.
Danaoi: Danaans.
Danaos: Descendant of Zeus and Io. Father of fifty daughters who fled from their cousins the Aigyptoi from Egypt to Argos.
Dardanian: Trojan, from Dardanos.
Dardanos: Son of Zeus and Elektra of Arkadia. Mythical ancestor of the Trojans.
Dawn: The goddess of Dawn (Eos). Daughter of Hyperion. Wife of Tithonos.
Deianeira: Wife of Herakles. Daughter of Oineus and Althaia. Sister of Meleager. Previously wooed by the river Acheloos and the cen-

taur Nessos, who gave her what he claimed was a love potion but was his own blood, poisoned by the arrow with which Herakles had killed the Hydra. With this potion Deianeira innocently killed Herakles.

Deinomenes: Father of Hiero, tyrant of Syracuse.

Deïphobos: A son of Priam and Hekabe. Slain by Menelaos after the fall of Troy.

Delian: Of Delos.

Delos: An Aegean island, birthplace of Artemis and Apollo.

Delphi: The famous sanctuary of Apollo in Phokis, central Greece.

Delphians: Inhabitants of Delphi.

Delphic: Of Delphi.

Demareta: A Spartan girl.

Demeter: Goddess of agriculture. Mother of Persephone. Sister of Zeus.

Demo: A daughter of Keleus and Metaneira.

Demophoön: Late-born son of Keleus and Metaneira.

Deo: A name of Demeter.

Diagoras: The Rhodian victor in the boxing match at Olympia in 464 B.C.

Dika: A young woman of Sappho's circle.

Dinnomenes: A friend of Alkaios.

Diokles: A prince of Eleusis.

Diomedes: One of the principal Greek heroes of the Trojan War.

Dionysos: Son of Zeus and Semele. God especially of wine but also of all the life force.

Dirkaion: Of Dirke, a fountain of Thebes.

Dog Star: Sirius.

Dolichos: A prince of Eleusis.

Dorian: A branch of the Greek race. Also the dialect spoken by those people. Sometimes it is used to mean "Spartan."

Doricha: A courtesan whose freedom Sappho's brother is said to have bought. Usually identified with the Rhodopis of Herodotus 2.135.

Doso: A name Demeter claims to be hers when she comes in disguise as an old woman to Keleus' house. It means "I will give."

Earthshaker: Poseidon.

Earth-upholder: Poseidon.

Echidna: A monster half-woman, half-serpent, who became by Typhon the mother of many horrible creatures including Kerberos, the "jag-toothed" hound who guarded Tartaros.

Echion: An Argonaut. Son of Hermes and Antianeira. Brother of Erytos.

Egypt: The country of North Africa.

Eilatos: 1. Father of Ischys, the lover of Koronis. 2. Father of Aipytos.

Eleithyia: Goddess of childbirth.

Elektra: In the *Hymn to Demeter* a nymph and playmate of Persephone. Daughter of Ocean and Tethys.
Eleusinians: The inhabitants of the city Eleusis.
Eleusis: A city of central Greece, northwest of Athens. Home of the Eleusinian mysteries.
Elis: A district of the northwestern Peloponnesos, where Olympia is located.
Endaïs: Wife of Aiakos, mother of Peleus and Telamon.
Enyalios: Epithet of Ares. Means "warlike."
Epaphos: Son of Zeus and Io. Born in Egypt. Father of Libya.
Epialtas: A giant. With his brother Otos he tried to reach heaven by piling Mount Ossa on Olympos and Mount Pelion on Ossa, but the brothers were slain by Apollo.
Epidauros: A town of Argolis in the Peloponessos. Famous for its sanctuary of Asklepios. Games in his honor were held there.
Erasmon: Father of Archilochos' friend Charilaos.
Eratidai: The clan to which Diagoras the victor belonged. They were the "sons of Eratos."
Erebos: The dark space through which shades pass into Hades. Often used for Hades itself.
Eriboia: 1. Mother by Telamon of Ajax. 2. The girl whose cheek Minos touched. In a later tradition she became Minos' wife.
Eritimos: Son of Terpsias. Nephew of Ptoiodoros. Relative of the victor Xenophon.
Eros: God of love. Son of Aphrodite by Ares, Zeus, or Hermes.
Erxias: A friend of Archilochos.
Erxion: An acquaintance of Anakreon.
Erysiche: A small town in Akarnania, west-central Greece.
Erytheia: A place in Spain.
Erytos: Son of Hermes and Antianeira. One of the Argonauts. Brother of Echion.
Etruscan: Of Etruria (modern Tuscany) in Italy.
Euboia: A long island off the east coast of central Greece.
Eumolpos: A prince of Eleusis.
Euonymos: Son of Kephisos and father of Aulis. A Boiotian prophet.
Euphamos: Son of Poseidon. An Argonaut.
Europa: Daughter of Tityos. Mother by Poseidon of Euphamos.
Eurotas: River near Sparta, southern Peloponessos.
Euryalos: A friend of Ibykos.
Eurypyle: A woman mentioned by Anakreon.
Eurypylos: One of the Tritons. Son of Poseidon.
Eurystheus: King of Tiryns who imposed upon Herakles his twelve labors and was slain by Iolaos in revenge.
Euxine: The Black Sea.
Evadne: Daughter of Poseidon and Pitana. Mother of Iamos.

Far-archer: Apollo.
Fates: Moirai, the daughters of Night. Represented as spinners. Their names were Klotho (Spinner), Lachesis (Apportioner), Atropos (Inflexible).
Flame: The name of a horse (Phlogeos) in Stesichoros 178.
Fury: Erinys, an avenging soul of the dead.
Gaia: Earth.
Galaxaura: A nymph and playmate of Persephone. Daughter of Ocean and Tethys.
Ganymede: Son of Tros. Zeus, enamored of his beauty, carried him off to be cupbearer to the gods.
Gastrodora: Perhaps a comic version of a woman's name. It seems to mean "belly-gift."
Geryon: A three-headed or three-bodied monster who lived in the far west (Spain) and was slain by Herakles. Stesichoros 186, however, gives him six hands, six feet, and wings.
Glaukos: 1. Son of Leptines. Friend of Archilochos. An aristocratic general, he was the most important political figure on Thasos and was given heroic honors there after his death. 2. A descendant of Bellerophon. In the Trojan War he fought on the Trojan side.
Gongyla: A young woman of Sappho's circle.
Gorgo: A woman who seems to have been a rival of Sappho.
Gorgon: Female monster with snake hair and a glance that turned mortals to stone. Medusa was the most famous of these. Pegasos sprang from her blood when Perseus beheaded her.
Graces: Lovely sisters, usually three in number, of divine, though variously given, parentage. Commonly associated with Aphrodite.
Gyaros: An island in the Aegean.
Gyges: King of Lydia, 685–57 B.C. He sent magnificent gifts to Delphi and his riches became proverbial.
Gyraian: Probably refers to the cliffs in the south of Tenos, an island in the Aegean.
Gyrinno: A young woman of Sappho's circle.
Hades: The underworld or the god thereof. Son of Kronos and Rhea. Brother of Demeter, Hera, Poseidon, and Zeus. Carried Persephone off to the underworld to be his bride.
Hagesias: Winner of the mule chariot race at Olympia in 427(?) B.C.
Hagesichora: A Spartan girl, apparently the leader of the chorus in Alkman 1. Her name means "choir leader."
Harmodios: An aristocratic Athenian who with Aristogeiton killed Hipparchos, brother of the tyrant Hippias, 514 B.C.
Harmonia: Daughter of Ares and Aphrodite. Wife of Kadmos. Mother of Semele and Ino.
Hebe: Goddess of youth. Daughter of Zeus and Hera.
Hebros: A river of Thessaly, northern Greece.
Hekate: Daughter of Persaios and Asterie. A goddess of the night, the

underworld, magic, crossroads, and graves. Sometimes identified with Artemis or the moon.

Hektor: Son of Priam. Husband of Andromache. The major Trojan hero of the Trojan War.

Helen: Daughter of Tyndareus (or of Zeus) and Leda. The most beautiful woman in the world and cause of the Trojan War.

Helenos: Son of Priam. A prophet.

Helikon: A mountain in Boiotia, home of the Muses.

Helios: The sun.

Hellas: Greece.

Hellenes: Greeks.

Hellotian: Refers to a torch race held in Corinth in honor of Athena Hellotis.

Hephaistos: God of fire. Son of Hera and husband of Aphrodite. Portrayed as a lame smith.

Hera: Daughter of Kronos and Rhea. Wife and sister of Zeus. Mother of Ares, Hephaistos, and Hebe.

Herakleidai: Descendants of Herakles.

Herakles: Son of Zeus and Alkmena. A favorite Greek hero known for his twelve labors.

Herald's Son: Translation of the Greek name, which is probably a made-up one.

Hermes: Son of Zeus and Maia. Born in a cave of Mount Kyllene in Arkadia. Herald of Zeus and guide of souls to Hades. Known for his cunning.

Hermione: Presumably a young woman of Sappho's circle.

Hero: Probably the name of a girl, though it may, according to one scholar, refer to the hero Lokrian Ajax, a good runner who was drowned near Gyrae.

Herotima: Apparently a woman of easy virtue.

Hesiod: Boiotian poet of about 700 B.C.

Hesperides: The daughter of Atlas and Hesperia. Guardians of the golden apples that Earth gave Hera upon her marriage to Zeus. Lived on Ocean in the extreme west.

Hestia: Daughter of Kronos and Rhea. Goddess of the hearth.

Hiero: Tyrant of Syracuse, 478–67 B.C. Patron of Aischylos, Pindar, and Bakchylides. Won many victories with his horses and chariots at the games.

Himera: A city on the north coast of Sicily. Site of a battle in 480 B.C. in which Theron of Akragas and Gelon of Syracuse defeated the Carthaginians.

Hipparchos: Brother of the Athenian tyrant Hippias. Slain by Harmodios and Aristogeiton in 514 B.C.

Hippodameia: Daughter of Oinomaos. Wife of Pelops.

Homer: The epic poet, author of the *Iliad* and the *Odyssey*.

Host of Many (Souls): Hades, who receives many in the underworld.

Hours: The Greek word *Horai* more accurately means "seasons." Often attendant upon Aphrodite.
Hydra: The water snake of nine (or more) heads slain by Herakles.
Hyllis: Mother of Zeuxippos, king of Sikyon, northern Peloponnesos, at the time of the Trojan War.
Hyllos: Son of Herakles and Deianeira. Founder of the Dorian tribe Hylleis.
Hymenaios: The god of marriage.
Hyperboreans: A fabulous people of antiquity. Supposed to live "beyond the north wind," which is what their name means.
Hyperian: Of Hyperia, a spring near Pherai in Thessaly, northern Greece.
Hyperion: A Titan, son of Ouranos (Heaven) and Gaia (Earth) and father of Helios (Sun), Selene (Moon), and Eos (Dawn).
Hypseus: King of the Lapithai and father of Kyrene.
Hyrieus: Son of Poseidon and Alkyone, father of Orion.
Hyrrhas: Father of the tyrant Pittakos.
Iache: A playmate of Persephone. Probably a nymph and one of the many daughters of Ocean and Tethys.
Ialysos: Grandson of Helios and Rhodes. Also a city of Rhodes.
Iambe: Daughter of Keleus and Metaneira.
Iamidai: Descendants of Iamos.
Iamos: Son of Evadne by Apollo. Legendary ancestor of the clan of Iamidai, who administered the oracle of Zeus' altar at Olympia. His name, Pindar, suggests, is derived from *ios,* the word for the bees' "venom," and from *ion,* the word for "violet."
Ianeira: A nymph and playmate of Persephone. Daughter of Ocean and Tethys.
Ianthe: A nymph and playmate of Persephone. Daughter of Ocean and Tethys.
Ianthemis: A Spartan girl.
Ibenian: Probably means "Lydian," referring to the country of Asia Minor.
Ida: 1. A mountain range of Mysia, Asia Minor. 2. A mountain in Crete in a cave of which Zeus was said to have been born.
Idaios: A herald of Troy.
Ilion: Troy.
Ilos: An ancestor of the Trojans. Grandfather of Priam. Was supposed to have founded Ilion, i.e., Troy.
Ino: After a stormy career, variously described, she jumped into the sea and was made "Queen of the Sea" by Dionysos (or Aphrodite) and called Leukothea. Best known as a sister of Semele and nurse of Dionysos.
Iolaos: Son of Iphikles, Herakles' mortal and twin brother. Took vengeance upon Eurystheus for the troubles he had brought upon Herakles. He was also a patron of athletic contests.

Iole: Princess of Oichalia in Euboia whom Herakles brought home as his bride.
Iolkos: An ancient town of Magnesia in Thessaly. The Argonauts departed from there.
Ionian Sea: The Adriatic, which lies between Greece and Italy.
Ionians: A branch of the Greek people, including Athenians.
Iphikles: 1. Althaia's brother. Meleager's uncle. 2. Herakles' mortal twin brother. Son of Amphitryon and Alkmena.
Iphimedeia: Mother by Poseidon of the giants Otos and Epialtas.
Irana: A young woman who evidently scorned Sappho.
Irasa: A city of Libya, north Africa.
Iris: A messenger of the gods. Often identified with the rainbow.
Ischys: Son of Eilatos. Lover of Koronis.
Ismarian: Of Ismaros in Thrace, northern Greece. Ismarian wine is probably what Archilochos drank on his campaign in Thrace.
Isthmian: Games held at the Isthmus of Corinth.
Isthmos: In *Olympian VII* the Isthmus of Corinth, central Greece.
Ixion: Father of the monster Kentauros. Punished in the underworld by being fixed to an ever-spinning wheel. The first man to shed kindred blood.
Jason: Son of Aison. Leader of the Argonauts.
Kadmeian: Theban, after Kadmos, its early king.
Kadmos: An early mythological king of Thebes. Father of Semele, who was the mother of Dionysos.
Kalais: Son of Boreas, the north wind. Brother of Zetes.
Kallianax: Ancestor of the victor Diagoras.
Kallichoros: A spring near the precinct of Eleusis.
Kallidike: A daughter of Keleus and Metaneira.
Kalliope: One of the nine Muses.
Kallirhoe: A nymph and playmate of Persephone. Daughter of Ocean and Tethys.
Kalliste: An early name for Thera. Means "most beautiful."
Kallithoe: A daughter of Keleus and Metaneira.
Kalydon: Town of Aitolia, west-central Greece.
Kalypso: In the *Hymn to Demeter* a nymph and playmate of Persephone. Daughter of Ocean and Tethys.
Kamiros: The grandson of Helios and Rhodes. Also a city of Rhodes.
Karneiadas: Father of Telesikrates.
Kassandra: Daughter of Priam and Hecuba. A prophetess.
Kastalia: A spring at Delphi.
Kastor: Son of Tyndareus. Brother of Polydeukes and Helen. Protector of sailors.
Kastorian: In *Pythian II* it seems to be a song celebrating a chariot victory.
Kean: Of the Aegean island Keos, home of Bakchylides.
Keleus: King of the city Eleusis, central Greece.

Kemelios: Dionysos. The meaning of the name is unknown.
Kenaian: Of Kenaion, the northwest promontory of Euboia, where there was a temple of Kenaian Zeus.
Kentauros: The monster born of Ixion's union with the cloud Hera. He was human above, horse below. The Magnesian Kentauros is, however, Chiron.
Kephisos: A river of Boiotia, central Greece.
Kerkyon: A villain who wrestled with passersby and killed the losers.
Kilikian: Refers to Kilikia, a district of Asia Minor, the birthplace of Typho.
Kinyras: A king of Kypros (Cyprus), the island in the Mediterranean famous for its perfume or hair oil.
Kirke: The famous sorceress. Daughter of Helios (the sun). She held Odysseus captive on her island Aiaia and turned his men to swine.
Kirrha: A town in the plain below Delphi. Pindar sometimes uses it to mean Delphi.
Kithairon: Mountain of Boiotia, central Greece. The battle before it in *Pythian I* is Plataia, 479 B.C.
Kleësithera: A Spartan girl.
Kleïs: Sappho's daughter.
Kleisidike: A daughter of Keleus and Metaneira.
Kleoboulos: 1. In Simonides 581 a poet of Rhodes, one of the Seven Wise Men, who wrote verses on Midas' tomb, to which Simonides here replies. 2. A friend and perhaps lover of Anakreon.
Klio: One of the nine Muses.
Klotho: One of the three Fates (Moirai). Her name means "spinner."
Klymenos: Son of Daïpylos. One of the Kouretes of Aetolia.
Knossian: Of the city Knossos on Crete.
Knossos: Chief city of Crete.
Koios: Father of Leto. Son of Ouranos (Heaven) and Gaia (Earth).
Koiranos: Father of Polyidos, a Corinthian seer.
Kokytos: A river of Epiros, northwest Greece; a tributary of Acheron and connected to the underworld. The name means "river of wailing."
Kolaxaian: Probably means "Skythian," referring to a people who lived north of the Caspian Sea and were famous for horsemanship.
Kolchian: Of Kolchis, a country at the far eastern end of the Black Sea.
Koralios: A river of Boiotia, central Greece.
Koronea: A city of Boiotia, central Greece.
Koronis: Daughter of Phlegyas. Mother by Apollo of Asklepios. Apollo destroyed her for lying with Ischys while pregnant with Asklepios.
Kouretes: 1. Demigods armed with brazen weapons to whom Rhea entrusted the infant Zeus for protection against Kronos. They drowned out the cries of the child by striking their spears against

their shields. 2. An Aitolian clan from Pleuron, west-central Greece.

Kremmyon: A place midway between Corinth and Megara, central Greece, where there was a man-eating sow.

Kreoisa: A naiad. Mother of Hypseus. Grandmother of Kyrene.

Kreousa: In *Dithyramb XVIII* mother of Aigeus, king of Athens.

Kretheus: Son of Aiolos. Brother of Salmoneus. Grandfather of Jason.

Kroisos: King of Lydia, 560–46 B.C. Defeated by Kyros, king of Persia. Famous for his wealth in gold.

Kronian: Of Kronos. Kronian Zeus means Zeus, son of Kronos.

Kronion: A hill of Kronos at Olympia.

Kronos: Son of Ouranos (Heaven) and Gaia (Earth). Father of Zeus, Hades, Poseidon, Hera, Demeter. Ruled in heaven until overthrown by Zeus.

Kydonian: Of Kydonia, a city of northwest Crete.

Kyke: Apparently the mother of Artemon.

Kyllene: A mountain of Arkadia in the Peloponnesos.

Kyllenian: Of Mount Kyllene in Arkadia, birthplace of Hermes.

Kyme: Cumae, a Greek settlement in Italy, near modern Naples.

Kyprian: Of Kypros (Cyprus), an island in the eastern Mediterranean particularly associated with Aphrodite; hence she is often called the Kyprian.

Kypris: Aphrodite.

Kypros: Cyprus, the Mediterranean island.

Kypros-born: Aphrodite.

Kyrene: A city of Libya, North Africa, and also the nymph whom Apollo loved and took to that city.

Kyrnos: The friend to whom Theognis addresses many of his poems.

Kythereia: Aphrodite, so-called from the island Kythera off the southeast point of Lakonia, the Peloponnesos, where she was worshipped from very early times.

Lachesis: One of the Three Fates (Moirai). Her name means "apportioner."

Lakedaimon: Sparta and the area surrounding it.

Lakereia: A town near Lake Boibios in Thessaly, northern Greece.

Lakonian: Of Lakonia, a province of the southern Peloponessos. Often used to mean Spartan.

Lampon: Father of the victor Pytheas.

Laomedon: King of Troy, son of Ilos, and father of Priam. It was for Laomedon that Poseidon built the walls of Troy.

Lapithai: A people of Thessaly, northern Greece. Famous for their battle with the centaurs.

Leda: Wife of Tyndareus. Mother by him of Klytemnestra and Kastor. Zeus made her mother of Helen and Polydeukes.

Lemnian: Of the Aegean island Lemnos.

Lemnos: An island in the Aegean. It once had an active volcano.
Leonidas: The Spartan king who held the pass at Thermopylai until he and his three hundred were slain.
Leophilos: An acquaintance of Archilochos.
Leptines: Father of Glaukos, the friend of Archilochos.
Lernaian: Of Lerna, a district on the coast of Argolis, where Herakles killed the Lernaian Hydra.
Lesbian: Refers to the island Lesbos.
Lesbos: An island in the Aegean, home of both Sappho and Alkaios.
Lethaios: A tributary of the Maeander River of Asia Minor. The city beside it in Anakreon 348 is Magnesia, where there was a temple of Artemis.
Leto: Mother by Zeus of Apollo and Artemis.
Leukadian cliff: A cliff at the southern tip of Leukas, an island in the Ionian Sea, from which Sappho is said to have thrown herself to death in her love for Phaon.
Leukaspis: A friend of Anakreon.
Leukippe: 1. A playmate of Persephone. Probably a nymph and one of the many daughters of Ocean and Tethys. 2. A woman mentioned by Anakreon.
Libya: A country of North Africa.
Likymnios: Son of Elektryon and his concubine Midea. Slain by Tlapolemos.
Lindos: Grandson of Helios and Rhodes. Also a city of Rhodes.
Lokrian: Refers to Lokris, a province of central Greece. In Alkaios 298 it refers to Ajax, the son of Oileus, who raped Kassandra in Athena's temple and was therefore drowned in a storm on his return voyage to Greece.
Loxias: An epithet of Apollo. Meaning uncertain.
Lykambes: Father of Neoboule. Supposedly a rich aristocrat of Paros.
Lydia: A country of Asia Minor.
Lykaios: Zeus, so-called from Mount Lykaion in Arkadia, where there was an altar of Zeus and where games were held in his honor.
Lykia: A country of Asia Minor.
Lykormos: A river of Aitolia, west-central Greece.
Lytaian: Epithet of Poseidon. Means "the loosener," supposedly because he opened the vale of Tempe in Thessaly to let the river Peneios through.
Magnesia: 1. A place in Thessaly, northern Greece. 2. A city of Caria in Asia Minor.
Magnesian: Of Magnesia in northern Greece.
Maia: Daughter of Atlas and Pleione. Eldest of the Pleiades and the most beautiful of the Seven Sisters. Mother by Zeus of Hermes.
Maiden Well: A well, not identified in modern times, in Eleusis.
Maids: In Ibykos 286 they are probably nymphs.
Malis: In Sappho or Alkaios 17 it may be a name for Athena.

Marathon: A district of Attica. Games were held there in honor of Herakles. Site of the famous battle of 490 B.C.

Medea: A sorceress. Daughter of the Kolchian king Aietes. Granddaughter of Helios. Helped Jason win the golden fleece and returned to Greece with him.

Medes: A people of Asia Minor conquered by the Persians, but the poets commonly use the word to mean the Persians.

Megalostrata: A Spartan woman with whom Alkman was reputed to have been passionately in love, but she may have been just an especially talented member of one of his choruses.

Megamedes: Father of Pallas who is named in the *Hymn to Hermes* as the father of Selene.

Megara: A city on the Isthmus of Corinth where games were held in honor of Alkathoos and Apollo.

Megatimos: Apparently a hero of the island Naxos.

Megistes: A friend of Anakreon.

Melampos: A seer. Cousin of Jason. Son of Amythan. One of the Argonauts.

Melanippos: A friend of Alkaios.

Meleager: Son of Oineus and Althaia. Grandson of Porthaon. One of the Argonauts. Famous for killing the Kalydonian boar.

Melian Sea: The Aegean south of the island of Melos.

Melite: A playmate of Persephone. Probably a nymph and one of the many daughters of Ocean and Tethys.

Melobosis: A nymph and playmate of Persephone. Daughter of Ocean and Tethys.

Memnon: Son of Tithonos and Eos (Dawn). King of the Aithiopians. Fought on Priam's side toward the end of the Trojan War.

Memory: Mnemosyne, mother by Zeus of the Muses.

Menander: The Athenian trainer of the victor Pytheas.

Menelaos: Son of Atreus. Brother of Agamemnon. Husband of Helen. One of the leaders of the expedition against Troy.

Menon: A friend, perhaps a lover, of Alkaios.

Messana: A district in the southwest Peloponnesos.

Metaneira: Wife of Keleus, the king of Eleusis.

Metope: A nymph of Stymphalos.

Midea: Concubine of Elektryon. Mother of Likymnios.

Milesians: People of Miletus, a city of Caria, Asia Minor.

Minos: Son of Zeus and Europa. King of Crete. After his death one of the judges in Hades.

Minyans: An ancient people of Boiotia living near Orchomenos. The word is often used for the Argonauts.

Mnasidika: A young woman of Sappho's circle.

Mnemosyne: Memory. Mother by Zeus of the Muses.

Molione: Mother of the charioteers Eurytos and Kteatos. Ibykos may be responsible for the tradition that they were Siamese twins.

Mopsos: A prophet and one of the Argonauts.
Muses: Daughters of Zeus and Memory. Patronesses of all the arts.
Mykenai: An ancient city of Argolis in the northeastern Peloponnesos.
Myrmidons: Earliest inhabitants of Aigina. They emigrated with Peleus to Thessaly. In the Trojan War they were Achilles' warriors.
Myrsilos: A tyrant of Mitylene whom Alkaios opposed.
Myrsineon: Perhaps a building named after Myrsilos.
Myrtis: A woman poet of Boiotia.
Mysians: The people of Mysia, a country of Asia Minor.
Mytilene: The most important city on the Aegean island Lesbos.
Nanno: A Spartan girl.
Naukratis: A city of northern Egypt. The garland of Naukratis is variously described as of marjoram, papyrus, lime, or myrtle.
Naxos: An island in the Aegean Sea.
Nemea: The place in Argolis where Herakles defeated the Nemean lion. Later the site of the Nemean games.
Neoboule: A girl whom Archilochos is supposed to have wanted to marry. He seems later to have scorned her.
Nereids: Sea nymphs. Daughters of Nereus and Doris.
Nereus: Son of Ocean and Earth. Father of the fifty Nereids (sea nymphs), including Thetis, the mother of Achilles. His wife was Doris.
Nessos: The wicked centaur who tried to ravish Deianeira and gave her the love potion, actually his own blood poisoned by the arrow with which Herakles had killed the Hydra. With the potion Deianeira inadvertently killed Herakles.
Nestor: Son of Neleus. King of Pylos. Father of Antilochos. An old man and hero who fought with the Greeks at Troy.
Nile: The great river of Egypt.
Niobe: A woman who boasted that she was superior to Leto because she had borne many children and Leto but two. Artemis and Apollo, Leto's children, therefore killed all but two of Niobe's children. Zeus then turned Niobe into a stone, which wept during the summer months, on Mount Sipylos in Lydia.
Nisos: King of Megara, whose daughter betrayed him to Minos. "Nisos' hill" means Megara, where games were celebrated.
Nomad: A Libyan tribe living near the city Irasa.
Nomios: Epithet of Aristaios. Means "herder."
Nysian: Name of a plain of unknown location.
Ocean: The river that surrounded the earth, often personified as the god of that river.
Odysseus: Hero of the Trojan War whose ten-year-long voyage home was the subject of Homer's *Odyssey*.
Oichalia: City of Euboia sacked by Herakles. Home of Iole.
Oidipous: King of Thebes who had solved the riddle of the Sphinx.

Married his own mother, killed his own father, and therefore blinded himself.

Oikleïdas: Son of Oikles, i.e., Amphiaraos.

Oineus: Father of Meleager.

Oinomaos: King of Pisa. Father of Hippodameia.

Okeanos: Ocean.

Okyroe: A nymph and playmate of Persephone. Daughter of Ocean and Tethys.

Oligaïthidai: Descendants of Oligaithos. The clan to which the victor Xenophon belonged.

Olympia: The site in Elis, western Peloponnesos, of the famous games.

Olympian: 1. Refers to Mount Olympos in Macedonia, northern Greece. 2. Refers to the games at Olympia in Elis.

Olympians: The gods who dwell on Mount Olympos.

Olympionician: Of Olympic victory.

Olympos: A mountain in Macedonia, northern Greece, believed to be the home of the gods.

Onchestos: A city of Boiotia, central Greece.

Onomakles: Presumably a recluse. Otherwise unknown.

Orion: Father of Akraiphen. Also the constellation.

Orpheus: Son of Apollo by Kalliope. Husband of Eurydike. A famous bard and one of the Argonauts.

Orthria: Presumably a goddess of dawn, though the spelling in the papyrus of Alkman 1 makes this uncertain. A vexed question.

Ortygia: An island near Syracuse. Site of the fountain Arethousa.

Otos: A giant who with his brother Epialtas planned to reach heaven by piling Mount Ossa on Olympos, Mount Pelion on Ossa. Both were slain by Apollo before they could do so.

Otreus: King of Phrygia, according to the lying tale Aphrodite tells Anchises.

Ourania: 1. In the *Hymn to Demeter* a nymph and playmate of Persephone. Daughter of Ocean and Tethys. 2. One of the Muses.

Ouranians: Dwellers in heaven, i.e., the gods.

Ouranidai: The offspring of Ouranos (Heaven).

Paian: A song to Apollo.

Paion: Apollo the Healer.

Paktolos: River of Lydia, famous for the gold dust it brought down from Mount Tmolos.

Pallas: 1. Father of Selene (Moon). 2. Athena.

Pamphylos: Son of Aigimios. Founder of the Dorian tribe of the Pamphyloi.

Pan: Son of Hermes. An Arkadian god of shepherds.

Pandion: King of Athens. Father of Philomela, who was turned into a swallow. Father of Aigeus. Grandfather of Theseus.

Pangaion: A mountain in Thrace, northern Greece.

Panormos: A city on the northern coast of Sicily.
Paphos: A town of Kypros, sacred to Aphrodite.
Paris: Son of Priam who stole Helen from Menelaos and so caused the Trojan War.
Parnassos: A mountain of Phokis, central Greece, sacred to Apollo and the Muses.
Paros: An island in the Aegean Sea.
Pasiphile: Probably a prostitute. Her name means "friendly to all."
Pegasos: Winged horse of Bellerophon. Born from Medusa's head when she was beheaded by Perseus.
Peirene: A fountain on the acropolis of Corinth.
Peleiades: The Pleiades or Doves. In Alkman 1 probably a rival chorus, though just possibly the constellation.
Peleus: Son of Aiakos. Husband of Thetis. Father of Achilles.
Pelian: Refers to Mount Pelion in Thessaly, northern Greece.
Pelias: Son of Tyro and Poseidon. Half-brother of Aison, Jason's father. King of Iolkos.
Pelion: A mountain of Magnesia in Thessaly, northern Greece.
Pellana: A town of Achaia, northern Peloponnesos. Games were held there, for which the prize was a woolen cloak.
Pelops: Grandson of Zeus. Son of Tantalos, the king of Phrygia. Married Hippodameia, daughter of Oinomaos, king of Elis. The Peloponnesos (island of Pelops) was named for him.
Peneios: A river of Thessaly, northern Greece.
Pergamon: Troy.
Perikles: A friend of Archilochos. (Not the famous statesman of Athens.)
Periklymenos: An Argonaut.
Persaios: A Titan. Father of Hekate.
Persephone: Daughter of Demeter and, like her, a goddess of agriculture. Carried off to the underworld by Hades.
Perseus: Son of Danae by Zeus, who came to her in a shower of gold. When Akrisios, her grandfather, discovered that she had given birth to a son who, it was prophesied, would destroy him, he put Danae and the infant Perseus into a chest and cast them into the sea. Perseus was the grandfather of Amphitryon and therefore the great-grandfather of Herakles.
Persians: The inhabitants of Persia, a major power in Asia during the late archaic and early classical periods.
Phaino: A playmate of Persephone. Probably a nymph and one of the many daughters of Ocean and Tethys.
Phaisana: A town on the river Alpheus, which flowed between Arkadia and Pisatis, western Peloponnesos.
Phalaris: Tyrant of Akragas, ca. 570–54 B.C., of notorious cruelty.
Phasis: A river of Kolchis, a kingdom at the eastern end of the Black Sea.

Pherenikos: Hiero's famous racehorse. Won in the Pythian games of 482 and 478 B.C. and in the Olympian games of 476 B.C. His name means "bringer of victory."

Pheres: Father of Admetos, king of Pherae in Thessaly. Uncle of Jason, who supported him in his attempt to regain the throne of Iolkos from Pelias.

Philoktetes: Son of Poias. Bitten by a snake on Lemnos and left there because of his festering foot by the Greeks on their way to Troy until they needed him to take the city.

Philylla: A Spartan girl.

Philyra: A daughter of Ocean. Mother by Kronos of the centaur Chiron.

Phintis: Driver of the mule cart for the Olympian victor Hagesias of Syracuse.

Phlegra: A place in Thrace, northern Greece, later called Pallene. Site of the battle between the giants and the gods.

Phlegyas: Son of Ares. Father of Koronis. King of the Lapithai.

Phoenix: Father of Europa, who was the mother of Minos.

Phoibos: An epithet of Apollo.

Phoinikian: Of Phoenicia, a country of Asia Minor. The Phoenicians were famous as sailors and traders. In *Pythian I* the word refers to Carthaginians. Carthage, a city of North Africa, was a Phoenician colony.

Phokaia: A city on the coast of Asia Minor.

Pholos: A centaur who entertained Herakles.

Phrixos: He rode the golden ram to safety in Kolchis. There he sacrificed it to Zeus and gave the fleece to Aietes.

Phrygia: A country of Asia Minor.

Phrygians: Inhabitants of Phrygia. In Alkaios 42 the word refers to the Trojans.

Phthia: A region of Thessaly and home of Achilles.

Pieria: District of the southeast coast of Macedonia, northern Greece. One of the earliest homes of the Muses, who were often called the Pierides.

Pierides: The Muses, so-called because they were associated with Pieria.

Pindos: A mountain range of northern Greece between Thessaly and Epiros.

Pisa: The district of the western Peloponnesos in which Olympia lay. Pindar often uses the word to mean Olympia or the Olympic games.

Pitana: 1. Daughter of the river Eurotas and mother of Evadne. 2. A town of Lakonia near Sparta, southern Peloponnesos.

Pittakos: A tyrant of Mytilene whom Alkaios opposed. He was also one of the Seven Wise Men of the ancient world.

Pittheus: Son of Pelops. King of Troezen. Father of Aithra. Grandfather of Theseus.
Plakia: Probably a river near Thebe, since a mutilated word in the papyrus seems to say "ever-flowing."
Pleiades: The constellation. They were the seven daughters of Atlas.
Pleisthenid: Refers to a descendant of Pleisthenes, the ancestor of Atreus, Thyestes, Agamemnon, Menelaos, and their children.
Pleuron: A city of Aitolia, west-central Greece.
Plouto: In the *Hymn to Demeter* a nymph and playmate of Persephone. Daughter of Ocean and Tethys.
Ploutos: Hades. The name means "wealth."
Poias: The father of Philoktetes.
Poliarche: The name is merely a conjecture. The manuscript seems to say something like "tender child."
Polyanax: Known only from Sappho 155. The ancient source for this quotation tells us that Sappho is here being ironic. The child of Polyanax may therefore be Gorgo or Andromeda.
Polydeukes: One of the Dioskuroi. Son of Tyndareus. Brother of Kastor and Helen. Protector of sailors.
Polykrates: In Ibykos 282, the son of the famous tyrant of Samos and himself a ruler of Rhodes.
Polymnastos: The father of Battos.
Polypemon: Apparently the father or predecessor of the Chopper (Prokoptes or Procrustes).
Polyxeinos: A prince of Eleusis.
Porthaon: King of Pleuron and Kalydon in Aitolia, west-central Greece, and grandfather of Meleager.
Poseidon: Son of Kronos and Rhea. Brother of Zeus. God of the sea and of earthquakes.
Priam: King of Troy during the Trojan War. Husband of Hekabe. Father of Hektor, Paris, Kassandra, etc.
Priene: A city on the coast of Asia Minor.
Ptoiodoros: Grandfather of the victor Xenophon.
Pylos: A city of Triphylia on the western coast of the Peloponnesos. Home of Nestor.
Pytheas: The Aiginetan victor at Nemea celebrated in Bakchylides, *Epinician XIII*.
Pythian: Of Pytho.
Pytho: Delphi, the seat of Apollo's oracle in Phokis, central Greece.
Pythomander: Unknown. Perhaps an acquaintance of Anakreon.
Ram: In Simonides 507 "Ram" refers to Krios (the word means "ram"), the famous Aiginetan wrestler. The fragment is from a victory song for him.
Rhadamanthys: Son of Zeus and Europa. A judge of the underworld.
Rharion: A place, not currently identified, in the vicinity of Eleusis.
Rhea: An earth goddess. Daughter of Ouranos (Heaven) and Gaia

(Earth). Wife of Kronos. Mother of Demeter, Hera, Hades, Poseidon, and Zeus.

Rhipe: Seems to refer to one of a range of mountains called Rhipaian, a name given rather indefinitely by Greek poets to mountains in the northern parts of Europe and Asia.

Rhodeia: A nymph and playmate of Persephone. Daughter of Ocean and Tethys.

Rhodes: The Mediterranean island and also the nymph, bride of Helios.

Rhodope: A nymph and playmate of Persephone. Probably one of the many daughters of Ocean and Tethys.

Saian: A member of a Thracian tribe from the mainland opposite the Aegean island Samothrace.

Salamis: A large island off Attica, central Greece. Home of Ajax, son of Telamon.

Salmoneus: Son of Aiolos. Father of Tyro. Grandfather of Pelias.

Salymydessos: A city on the eastern coast of Thrace, northern Greece.

Samos: An island in the Aegean Sea.

Sappho: The poet.

Sardis: The capital of Lydia, Asia Minor.

Sarpedon: Son of Zeus. A Lykian ally of the Trojans.

Selene: The moon. Sister of Helios, the sun.

Semele: Mother by Zeus of Dionysos.

Seven Stars: The Pleiades.

Sicily: The large island of the Mediterranean. A Greek settlement.

Sikyon: A city west of Corinth where games were held.

Silenoi: Satyrlike creatures. Associated with Dionysos. Often portrayed as lecherous.

Silver-bowed: Apollo.

Simalos: A friend of Anakreon.

Simonides: 1. A friend of Theognis. 2. The poet.

Sinis: A villain who operated at the Isthmus of Corinth. He tied his victims arms to two bent pine trees, which he then released.

Sipylos: A city of Lydia, Asia Minor. The site of Tantalos' banquet for the gods.

Siren: A bird-woman whose song was so high-pitched and sweet that it caused sailors to run aground.

Siris: A river of southern Italy.

Sirius: The Dog Star.

Sisyphos: Son of Aiolos. He was allowed to return to earth from Hades to reproach his wife for failing to oversee his funeral rites. Eventually he died again from old age. Upon reaching Hades for the second time he was condemned to roll a stone to the top of a hill from which it would always roll down again. He was also the founder of Corinth and known for his cunning.

Skiron: A robber who made travelers wash his feet and kicked them over the Skironian cliffs near Corinth as they did so.

Skythians: Skyths.
Skyths: Skythians, a nomadic people living to the north of the Black and Caspian seas. Known for their horsemanship.
Smerdis: A friend of Anakreon.
Snatcher: Name of a horse (Harpagos) in Stesichoros 178.
Solymoi: A people who lived between Lykia and Pamphylia in Asia Minor.
Sostratos: Father of the Olympic victor Hagesias of Syracuse.
Sparta: A city of Lakonia, southern Peloponnesos.
Spartoi: "Sown men," sprung from the dragon's teeth sown by Kadmos.
Stesichoros: The choral poet.
Strattis: An acquaintance of Anakreon.
Stymphalian: Refers to Stymphalos, a town of Arkadia, Peloponnesos. Hagesias' maternal ancestors had come from there.
Styx: River of the underworld. Oaths sworn by it were especially strong. In the *Hymn to Demeter* a nymph and playmate of Persephone. The most important of the daughters of Ocean and Tethys.
Sylakis: A Spartan girl.
Syracusan: Of Syracuse.
Syracuse: The principal city of Sicily.
Tainaron: A Lakonian city near Cape Tainaron at the tip of Tainaron, the central peninsula of the southern Peloponnesos.
Talaos: Father of Adrastos.
Tantalos: Son of Zeus. Father of Pelops. His punishment in the underworld was to have a boulder forever suspended over his head.
Targelios: Presumably an acquaintance of Anakreon.
Tartaros: Hades or the underworld.
Tartessos: A district, a river, and a town of Spain. Originally a Phoenician settlement.
Taÿgetos: A high mountain range of Lakonia overlooking Sparta.
Teian: Of Teos, a city of Ionia on the coast of Asia Minor.
Teiresias: The famous blind seer of Thebes.
Telamon: Father of the greater Ajax.
Telamonian: Of Telamon. Telamonian Ajax means Ajax, son of Telamon.
Telesikrates: The Kyrenian victor in the footrace in full armor at the Pythian games in 474 B.C.
Terpsias: A relative of the victor Xenophon.
Thasos: An island in the northern Aegean. Archilochos' father, Telesikles, helped to found a Parian colony there, and Archilochos himself eventually settled there.
Thearion: The guild hall of the sacred ambassadors sent from Aigina to Delphi.
Thebe: 1. City near Troy sacked by Achilles. Home of Andromache. 2. Eponymous nymph of Thebes. Daughter of Asopos and Metope.

Thebes: The chief city of Boiotia, central Greece.

Themis: Daughter of Ouranos (Heaven) and Gaia (Earth). Her name means "order." Mother by Zeus of the nymphs.

Thera: An island in the Aegean now called Santorini. People from there colonized Kyrene.

Thermopylai: The pass in Thessaly, northern Greece, which was the site of the famous battle of the Persian Wars.

Theseus: Son of Aigeus, king of Athens, and of Aithra, daughter of Pittheus, king of Troezen. Slew many monsters and was a major Athenian hero.

Thessalian: Of Thessaly.

Thessalos: Father of the victor Xenophon.

Thessaly: A district in northern Greece.

Thestios: Father of Althaia.

Thetis: Daughter of Nereus. Wife of Peleus. Mother of Achilles.

Thoas: Not actually in Pindar's text. I supplied the name for clarity's sake. Thoas was the father of Hypsipyle, the Lemnian queen who particularly welcomed Jason.

Thorikos: A place north of Cape Sounion at the southern tip of Attica, central Greece.

Thrace: A district of northern Greece.

Thracian: Of Thrace.

Thyone: Semele.

Tiryns: A city of Argolis, the Peloponnesos.

Tirynthian: Refers to the city of Tiryns.

Titans: Children of Heaven and Earth. The generation of gods preceding the Olympians. Ocean, Kronos, Rhea, Hyperion were among them.

Tithonos: The husband of Dawn (Eos).

Tityos: Son of Zeus and Elara. A giant who attempted to rape Leto and was therefore slain by Artemis. Pindar makes him the father of Europa.

Tlapolemos: Son of Herakles and Astydameia. He killed his maternal granduncle Likymnios and so Apollo's oracle advised him to leave Tiryns and colonize Rhodes.

Triptolemos: In the *Hymn to Demeter* one of the local princes. Later he became an important figure in the Eleusinian mysteries. In later authorities a son of Keleus and Metaneira.

Tritogeneia: A name for Athena. Meaning unknown.

Tritonian: Of Lake Tritonis in Libya.

Troezen: A city of Argolis, northeastern Peloponnesos.

Troilos: A son of Priam.

Trojans: Inhabitants of Troy.

Tros: Grandson of Dardanos, the mythical ancestor of the Trojans. Father of Ganymede.

Troy: City on the Hellespont in Asia Minor (on the Dardanelles in modern Turkey). Site of the Trojan War.
Tyche: A nymph and playmate of Persephone. Daughter of Ocean and Tethys.
Tydeus: Father of Diomedes.
Tyndareus: Father of Klytemnestra and mortal father of Helen.
Tyndaridai: The sons of Tyndareus, Kastor and Polydeukes. Patrons of athletic games. Tutelary heroes at Olympia.
Typho: A monster, son of Earth and Tartaros. He once tried to usurp the power of Zeus and so lies pinned beneath Mount Aitna in Sicily.
Tyro: Daughter of Salmoneus. Mother by Poseidon of Pelias.
Tyrrakean: Meaning unknown. The text is in doubt.
Tyrsenia: In the *Hymn to Dionysos* probably Etruria (modern Tuscany) in Italy, famous for its pirates.
Undercutter: A worm that was supposed to cause toothache.
Venetic: In Alkman 1 it is uncertain whether this refers to the horses of Paphlagonia on the southern shore of the Black Sea or to those of the northern Adriatic in Italy.
Whitefoot: Name of a horse (Podarge) in Stesichoros 178.
Xanthos: A river of Lykia or of the Troad in Asia Minor.
Xenophon: The Corinthian victor in the footrace and pentathlon at Olympia in 464 B.C.
Zephyros: The west wind.
Zetes: Son of Boreas, the north wind. Brother of Kalais.
Zeus: King of the gods. Son of Kronos. Husband and brother of Hera.

SELECT BIBLIOGRAPHY

Athanassakis, A. *The Homeric Hymns*. Baltimore and London, 1976.

Bowra, C. M. *Early Greek Elegists*. Cambridge, Mass., 1938.

Bowra, C. M. *Greek Lyric Poetry from Alcman to Simonides*. 2d rev. ed. Oxford, 1961.

Bowra, C. M. *Pindar*. Oxford, 1964.

Burnett, A. P. *Three Archaic Poets: Archilochus, Alcaeus, Sappho*. Cambridge, Mass., 1983.

Burnett, A. P. *The Art of Bacchylides*. Cambridge, Mass., and London, 1985.

Campbell, D. A. *The Golden Lyre: The Themes of the Greek Lyric Poets*. London, 1983.

Clay, J. S. *The Politics of Olympus: Form and Meaning in the Major Homeric Hymns*. Princeton, N.J., 1989.

Crotty, K. *Song and Action: The Victory Odes of Pindar*. Baltimore and London, 1982.

Fagles, R. *Bacchylides: Complete Poems*. New Haven, Conn., and London, 1961.

Fowler, B. H., "The Centaur's Smile: Pindar and the Archaic Aesthetic." In *Ancient Greek Art and Iconography*, ed. W. G. Moon. Madison, Wis., 1983.

Fowler, B. H. "The Archaic Aesthetic." *American Journal of Philology 105* (1984): 119–49.

Fowler, B. H. "Constellations in Pindar." *Classica et Mediaevalia 37* (1986): 21–46.

Fränkel, H. *Early Greek Poetry and Philosophy*, trans. M. Hadas and J. Willis. Oxford, 1975.

Kirkwood, G. M. *Early Greek Monody*. Ithaca, N.Y., 1974.

Lattimore, R. *The Odes of Pindar*. Chicago, 1947.

Lefkowitz, M. *The Victory Ode: An Introduction*. Park Ridge, N.J., 1976.

Lefkowitz, M. *The Lives of the Greek Poets*. Baltimore, 1981.

Mullen, W. *Choreia: Pindar and the Dance*. Princeton, N.J., 1982.

Nisetich, F. J. *Pindar's Victory Songs*. Baltimore and London, 1980.

Norwood, G. *Pindar*. Berkeley and Los Angeles, 1945.

Page, D. *Sappho and Alcaeus*. Oxford, 1955.

Richardson, N. J. *The Homeric Hymn to Demeter*. Oxford, 1974.

Wisconsin Studies in Classics

General Editors
Barbara Hughes Fowler and Warren G. Moon

E. A. Thompson
Romans and Barbarians: The Decline of the Western Empire

Jennifer Tolbert Roberts
Accountability in Athenian Government

H. I. Marrou
A History of Education in Antiquity
Histoire de l'Education dans l'Antiquité, translated by George Lamb
(originally published in English by Sheed and Ward, 1956)

Erika Simon
Festivals of Attica: An Archaeological Commentary

G. Michael Woloch
Roman Cities: Les villes romaines by Pierre Grimal,
translated and edited by G. Michael Woloch,
together with A Descriptive Catalogue of Roman Cities by G. Michael Woloch

Warren G. Moon, *editor*
Ancient Greek Art and Iconography

Katherine Dohan Morrow
Greek Footwear and the Dating of Sculpture

John Kevin Newman
The Classical Epic Tradition

Jeanny Vorys Canby, Edith Porada, Brunilde Sismondo Ridgway,
and Tamara Stech, *editors*
Ancient Anatolia: Aspects of Change and Cultural Development

Ann Norris Michelini
Euripides and the Tragic Tradition

Wendy J. Raschke, *editor*
The Archaeology of the Olympics: The Olympics and Other Festivals in Antiquity

Paul Plass
Wit and the Writing of History: The Rhetoric of Historiography in Imperial Rome

Barbara Hughes Fowler
The Hellenistic Aesthetic

F. M. Clover and R. S. Humphreys, *editors*
Tradition and Innovation in Late Antiquity

Brunilde Sismondo Ridgway
Hellenistic Sculpture I: The Styles of ca. 331–200 B.C.

Barbara Hughes Fowler, *editor and translator*
Hellenistic Poetry: An Anthology

Kathryn J. Gutzwiller
Theocritus' Pastoral Analogies: The Formation of a Genre

Vimala Begley and Richard Daniel De Puma, *editors*
Rome and India: The Ancient Sea Trade

Barbara Hughes Fowler, *editor and translator*
Archaic Greek Poetry: An Anthology

David Castriota
Myth, Ethos, and Actuality: Official Art in Fifth-Century B.C. *Athens*